TALES OF THE TURQUOISE

A Pilgrimage in Dolpo

TALES OF THE TURQUOISE

A *Pilgrimage in Dolpo*

by
Corneille Jest

translated from the French by
Margaret Stein

Snow Lion Publications
Ithaca, New York

Snow Lion Publications
P.O. Box 6483
Ithaca, New York 14851 USA
Tel: 607-273-8519

ISBN 1-55939-095-6

Printed in Canada on recycled paper.

Library of Congress Cataloging-in-Publication Data

Jest, Corneille.
   [Turquoise de vie. English]
   Tales of the turquoise : a pilgrimage in Dolpo / Corneille Jest ; translated from the French by Margaret Stein.
      p. cm.
   Includes index.
   ISBN 1-55939-095-6 (alk. paper)
   1. Buddhist pilgrims and pilgrimages--Nepal--Dolpā. 2. Tibetans--Folklore. 3. Tales--China--Tibet. 4. Tales--Nepal. 5. Dolpā (Nepal)--Religious life and customs. I. Stein, Margaret.
BQ6450.N352D655 1998
398.2'0951'5--dc21   98-5357
                                                       CIP

Table of Contents

List of Karma's Stories

Acknowledgments

La turquoise de vie was originally published in French in 1985. It has been translated by Margaret Stein. I am grateful to her as well as to Ethan Stein and Manjula Padmanabhan for bringing this edition to reality. Alex Berzin assisted with the translation of religious terms.

Special thanks to Kungya, a monk of Tarap, for making the drawings for this book. In traditional Tibet, painting was solely a religious vocation, governed by very strict rules as to choice of elements, their arrangement, and the colors used. Today, graphic art is finding broader usage, particularly for illustration of non-religious texts. This transformation is exemplified in the drawings prepared for this book.

— *To Shungru Karma, with deepest gratitude* —

Foreword

When one learns without a Master,
One's knowledge is without roots.

Keeping this frequently heard Tibetan proverb in mind, I would like to introduce Karma, a nomad of Tibet, my friend and travelling companion. To this wise man, more than to anyone else, I owe my understanding of the Tibetan spirit. I consider myself fortunate, from the human as well as the professional points of view, to have made the acquaintance of Karma—a man of maturity and experience who was sympathetic and trusting toward someone whose motives must have appeared incomprehensible.

Karma was an excellent travelling companion and I was lucky to have been able to visit most of Dolpo in his company. Karma was also a natural storyteller. He was always happy to speak and his stories were often spontaneous responses to incidents on the road, to an encounter with an animal, to a special landscape, to a comment from a listener. While Karma was not a professional storyteller, he was nevertheless a gifted raconteur who greatly enjoyed this pastime and I consider myself to have been particularly fortunate to have been present during numerous occasions when he told tales from his vast repertoire. There was never any intention on Karma's part to teach, nor any desire to express personal sentiments or ideas. Also, Karma did not appear to be motivated by any desire to convey to the younger ones the stock of stories and folk-sayings accumulated in the course of his long life. Karma had then an opportunity to deliver a message, the story becoming an expression of a code of values, of Tibetan customs and manners. And my desire, first as a listener and then as a writer, is to introduce the reader to the mental world of the Tibetan—layman, yak herder—pious to his deities and divinities with whom he seemed to talk freely, sensitive to an invisible world to which he related with his divinations and his invocations.

To a Westerner, the risk of losing the cultural treasures lying with this elderly man seemed very real, all the more so as it seemed clear that the way of life necessary for the preservation of the thousand-year-old tradition they belong to was itself now threatened. But if these perspectives for the future or, indeed, any awareness of the prospects for radical changes were among Karma's thoughts, he never made any hint, nor did he show any curiosity with regard to the Western way of life.

If the individuality of the storyteller did not make itself felt in the substance of the story, it was, however, expressed in the tone of voice the teller adopted, in the change of tone and rhythm corresponding to situations being described, in the importance given to silence, in the use made of questions and exclamations, in casual recollections made in the middle of a narration on the occasion of an incident such as a sudden and heavy downpour of rain, the flight of a bird, etc.

Karma's stories, free of any intention of eloquence, were nonetheless delivered with some desire to inform, possibly due to a belief that the relating of adventures whose meaning was in some way edifying would earn merit for the teller.

Karma, like most Tibetans, appeared to demonstrate a wish to impress upon the minds of his listeners the effects of sudden turns of fortune. Thought-provoking themes, common sayings

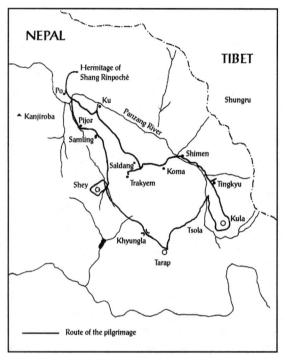

NEPAL

TIBET

Hermitage of
Shang Rinpoché

Kanjiroba

Po

Ku

Pijor

Samling

Shungru

Panzang River

Saldang

Koma

Shimen

Shey

Trakyem

Tingkyu

Kula

Tsola

Khyungla

Tarap

—————— Route of the pilgrimage

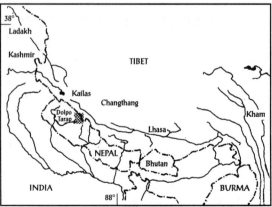

38°

Ladakh

Kashmir

TIBET

Kailas

Changthang

Dolpo
Tarap

Kham

Lhasa

NEPAL

Bhutan

INDIA

88°

BURMA

and proverbs often mark the main points. The telling was not without a certain monotony, but this was neither disappointing nor boring, and is in fact a part of the style of storytelling in many cultures.

At times the reader may have difficulty identifying the characters. If so, this is due to the absence of personal names of the characters in many of the stories. It is the same for the names of places.

As to the gestures of the storyteller, they are restrained— only the left hand moving the beads of a rosary. Tibetans are seldom inclined to speak with their hands.

It is also necessary to be aware of the role of the collector of the stories and of the factors involved in the translation into French (and then English) of that which belongs to an essentially spoken language, with its own unique grammar, idiom and vocabulary. An attempt has been made to convey the Tibetan sense of time and space and to exclude the precision and the sense of haste which are familiar in the West. I have tried to present the characters of the fables as the storyteller depicted them, without making them more interesting or colorful for the reader. If they appear stereotyped, this is the price of authenticity. My endeavor has been to show the day-to-day life in a way that reveals the richness of the Tibetan mental world.

This pilgrimage took place the year of the Iron Ox, 1961 A.D.

Karma the Pilgrim

Coral—flower of a marvelous tree.
Turquoise—treasure of the water divinities.

My friend Karma the *drogpa*, Norbu and I are ready to set off on our pilgrimage. Friends and well-wishers have come to see us off. Karma and Norbu wear *chubas* that are almost new and they each have a reliquary slung over the shoulder and a rosary around the left wrist. Kagar Rinpoché, the Precious Teacher of Kagar, is wrapped in his fur-lined coat. His long matted hair is piled on the top of his head and wrapped around like a turban. The women of Kagar have interrupted their weaving. With heads raised over the wall of the courtyard where they are working, they watch and talk.

Kagar Rinpoché adds some twigs of juniper to the container placed on the wall facing the temple, making an offering of incense. Domnag, "Black Bear," a Tibetan mastiff, so named because of his size and color, barks with all his might and pulls at his chain; he senses something unusual.

We are finally ready for the *lingkhor* of Dolpo.

It all began several days earlier in Karma's tent. He had only just changed tents, folding away the winter one made of yak hair and erecting a small summer one of white cotton a little way up the hill, near the houses of Kagar. Seated around the hearth were Karma, Tsorpön Angdü, Norbu, Chögya Tondrup the painter, Chöwang, Lama Jamyang, Lama Urgyen Gyaltsen of Kagar, and myself. Almost everyone there was playing dice, and Karma had just ended a run. Urgyen Gyaltsen did not play, but had drunk much *chang*. As for Lhaki, Karma's wife, she was seated somewhat aside, kneading the fermented barley that she then mixed with water and stirred into a large basin with a willow twig to make the beer.

We had been discussing the condition of the herds and the pastures. Lhaki served the beer; a ladleful just filled a wooden tea bowl. She came back to the hearth and put on the teapot after feeding the fire, placing chips of yak dung carefully one upon the other.

There was a silence; there is always silence in the tent when the fire tells of a brewing in the teapot. Then the conversation revived and we came to the subject of pilgrimages. Karma and Tsorpön Angdü began recalling their memories of their pilgrimages to Kang Tisé in Western Tibet, where they had gone many times.[1] Being then in the second part of the Fifth Month, the time of the *nékhor* of Shey, Karma, Norbu and I decided to go to Shey and continue on from there and visit all the sacred places of Dolpo. It was late in the night and we began working out the plans for our departure and our route.

We later discussed the itinerary at length with Kagar Rinpoché, who encouraged us and added, when speaking to me, that I would understand the customs better: "Did I not come for this purpose?" Turning to Karma, Rinpoché remarked to him that most of the people of the community did not have the time to make this tour, and that we would acquire merit for them also. Finally, on his advice, the most favorable day for departure was fixed: "The 28th day of this month, preferably early in the morning."

Up till this time I had already had many meetings with Kagar Rinpoché. Evening after evening he would receive me in his personal chapel. Through him, I came to understand the history of Dolpo. His chapel was a tiny room on the first floor of the temple of Kagar. There, he spends his days without going out, seated or lounging on a low couch, half chair, half bed; a small plain table serves for placing his bowl of tea or a book.

At the beginning of my stay in Dolpo, Kagar Rinpoché's dog, a small apso with a reddish coat, would bark when I entered. Later on, the dog stopped barking at me and would remain at his master's feet, resting comfortably in the warmth of a fold of his master's fur-lined coat. Then I would take a seat on the carpet, facing the altar, to await the waking of Kagar Rinpoché. Kagar Rinpoché would raise himself, putting his hair in order; always the same movement of the hands, always a short prayer. He would ring a little bell to ask for some tea and *tsampa*. Then we would talk....

I was having a lot of trouble with the terms of the religious vocabulary; it was all new to me and I was searching for specific facts with which to support the chronology of events, to place the historic sites and the temples in their proper context. Kagar Rinpoché would respond in terms of the wonderful, the supernatural. He inherited his knowledge from his father, a lama, who had educated him. His father taught him by reading and analyzing the texts of the Nyingma sect. He also taught him painting. But it was, above all, the Precious Teacher of Shang who helped him to go deeply into the doctrine, through his commentaries on the sacred texts. Kagar Rinpoché, in turn, transmitted the teachings he had received to Mémé Tenzin, his younger brother, to whom he was tied by special bonds: Kagar Rinpoché, at the age of thirty, had decided to withdraw from worldly life in order to meditate and he had entrusted his wife to his younger brother, an accepted practice, by whom she had a son, Urgyen Gyaltsen, who in his turn became a lama.

Now a widower, Mémé Tenzin is very active in spite of his sixty-five years and still participates in all the religious ceremonies as well as the public reading of sacred texts. A reputed *amchi*, he spends much time gathering medicinal plants and preparing medications. This gives him an opportunity to go far from home. With his loquacious nature, he dearly loves to speak about the practice of his skill, all the while trying to locate some item from within a multitude of little skin pouches, each one containing a vegetable or mineral substance which he grinds on a stone plate with a river-washed pebble. His diagnosis is reputed to be unfailing, and when his medicine has no effect, Mémé Tenzin puts the cause on local demons or on the *lu*, divinities of the springs.

Our preparations began. Lhaki brought out thirty measures of barley to use for making *tsampa* for us to eat along the way, and Karma and Norbu repaired the stitching of their boots. Soles of yak hide have frequent need of being repaired, and they will apply themselves to this frequently during our tour.

A whole day was spent on the roof of a Kagar house in printing prayer flags on white, red and blue kerchief-sized squares of cotton fabric. This was done by pressing the fabric against inked wooden boards which have ornamented motifs and religious invocations carved on one side. These *lungtas* are to be attached to stakes, or wedged under stones, along the sides of passes over which our itinerary will lead us.

Konchog Gyaltsen, the smith, was called to sharpen the various awls necessary for the work of sewing leather. A leather bag holds his entire stock of tools. When it is necessary to fabricate or repair something, he sets up his "workshop" under the portal of a house, choosing a big stone for an anvil and scooping out a cavity in the earth to make the hearth. With a blow pipe of potter's clay and his goat-skin bellows, he gets down to his craft. I saw one of his silver pieces on a woman of Dolpo, a long clasp of worked silver resembling a butterfly with outspread wings. Like an itinerant magic show, he always has a crowd around him while working, as he knows how to collect and how to pass on the news of the place. He stops from time to time to drink a bowl of tea or *chang* and to drop a few decisive remarks that would feed, or shut off, the gossip. The thorny, if not improper, questions that he would raise are summed up in the proverb: "Never put a yak and a *dri* under the same yoke; besides working, Chogya beds down with Yingji and pleases himself well with her."

One last time before our departure we pay a visit to Kagar Rinpoché. He offers us tea, gives us more information about places to see, and requests us to bring back stones from the various sacred sites we will visit. Then he hands Karma a turquoise, saying, "I entrust this *la-yü* to you, which all men wear as a stone of luck and good omens. Of all riches, this is the most precious; it protects and it cures. At the end of your pilgrimage, which will go well, I am sure of it, you will return home with all the blessings accumulated on the way."

In Tibetan culture, the turquoise, *yü*, has a particularly profound symbolic value. Being both a "living" stone and susceptible to destruction, it shares with humans a common destiny. It represents both vitality and death. It also represents both beauty and wealth and serves as a "support" to human life itself. The term *la-yü* (literally "vital-spirit turquoise") occurs frequently in mythical and legendary themes and in folk tales: *la* referring to the vital spirit that humans are believed to possess, the will to live, the ability to function as an integrated person. It is this spirit or force that a turquoise guards, conserves, protects and supports.

There are numerous rituals capable of retrieving the *la*, the vital spirit, should the *la* abandon the body. Karma had recounted to me a characteristic scene of a ritual, to which he had been a witness: On the large plain to the north, a woman was ill and a medium, *lhapa*, was called. The *lhapa* placed a clean copper cooking pot on the hearth, heated by three pieces of yak dung. He then poured into the pot some pure water blessed by the *lu* and some milk from a blue-haired goat (*dri* milk or the milk of a blue-haired ewe, or the milk of a woman, would have served just as well). At the bottom of the pot, the *lhapa* placed the sick person's turquoise, then covered the pot with a piece of white silk. Then, once the tutelary deity (*yidam*) of the *lhapa* had taken possession of him, his assistant picked up the turquoise, wrapped it in *tsampa* dough, and handed it to the sick one, who, using a sling "with nine eyes," flung it away. The medium entered into a trance and, through magic power, caused the turquoise to return to the pot. Such is the power of the *la-yü!* "If it does not return to its place of starting," added Karma, "the sick one dies."

With regard to the concept of the turquoise as a *sog kyob*, a life-protecting object mentioned in Tibetan medical texts, the turquoise is believed to contain the energy present in the human body which can escape at any time, particularly from the little finger. The body is exposed to all kind of dangers, above all to ill-treatment by malevolent spirits (to which small children are particularly vulnerable) and this explains why Tibetans wear a turquoise around the neck.

Turquoises are similar to people; they live and they die. Their efficacy is linked to quality, and it is said that the most precious belong to one of three types: *yü trugsé*, those which are the color of the heavens, white and pale blue; *yü trugkar*, those which are blue and white; and most valuable of all, *yü trugmar*, those which are blue with veins of red and black and which come from lakes, which are the treasury of the *lu*, the protectors of lakes and springs.

The turquoise is also much worn as an ornament. When worn at the top of the head, it expresses a common saying, taken from the marriage ritual: "In the mouth, the good taste of tea; at the top of the head, a turquoise." The turquoise is often seen mounted as an element of decoration in the silver jewelry worn in everyday life—men's earrings, a man's belt buckle, or as a woman's brooch.

The color of turquoise-blue is the color that the Guardian Lioness is adorned with; it is a supremely noble color.

Waking up on the day of our departure, we are many and we collect under Karma's tent.

Karma is of medium height, almost bald, and has lost most of his teeth, which gives him the appearance of an old man. He always wears a felt hat which he bought at the market in Purang.

Karma is a *drogpa*, and he hails from Shungru, just over the border. *Drogpas* are nomadic breeders of yaks and sheep and populate the highest elevations of the regions of Tibetan culture. For a long time, the fifty-odd "tent-holds" of Shungru, spread over an area of many square kilometers, have maintained barter-trade relations with the valleys of Dolpo. Karma, whose father had been head of the Shungru nomads, however, settled down with his family near Kagar and looks after the flocks of Kagar Rinpoché.

Karma has the reputation of being an excellent breeder of yaks and horses. Though he may not know how to read or write, he knows the omens and the various forms of divining (*mo gyab*) with the rosary, with the shoulder blade of a sheep, with salt, with the sling, and with the boot garter string (*lhamdrog*). He treats the animals when they fall sick and for this he possesses an assortment of protective charms. Kagar Rinpoché does not hesitate to ask his advice regarding the protection of the herds. "The lamas," says Karma, "are powerless before the forces of nature." As leader of a caravan he has made many journeys to the west as well as to the center of Tibet.

The second companion of the road, Norbu, is just twenty years old. He comes from Kyirong, a Tibetan center of trade to the north of Kathmandu. His parents were serfs attached to a monastery, looking after the mill, and had very few personal possessions. His father had three wives in succession. Norbu, abused by a stepmother, left home. A tall man, he has cut his long braids and always wears trousers and *chuba* of finely woven black wool. With his striking appearance, Norbu stands out from the other men of Dolpo. Possessing an alert and inquiring mind, he is very familiar with the world of nature and has been, like me, an enthusiastic listener to him whom we quickly came to refer to as *Agu* Karma.

At last we are ready. Norbu puts the sack of *tsampa* in his pack, as well as a sack of wheat flour, a ball of tea, a lump of butter sewn up in goat skin, some salt, some dried chillies, and a pot for making tea. Karma rolls his things in the fly-sheet of a tent which, folded, he carries by means of a rope over his shoulders.

We begin our pilgrimage.

Karma wants to offer a butter lamp to the statue of Champa, the "Buddha of the Future."[2] The temple of Champa is located in the middle of the inhabited part of the valley, between *do*, the low, and *uma*, the high. Of the original construction, only a group of eight *chörten* now remain, which have been protected by a small rectangular structure. The temple itself was rebuilt some years ago, with everyone lending a hand. The walls are of stones gathered from the bed of the nearby stream and the beams and small joists of fir came from Reng, from where they were transported on the backs of yaks. In the entrance are the traditional paintings that one always lingers to look at: "The Wheel of Life" which reminds one of the uncertainties of the rounds of existence; the Guardian Kings of the Four Directions and the traditional symbols of long life—the old man who is making an offering, the pair of cranes, the pine tree, the cliff, the waterfall and the antelope. The Assembly Hall, built to a square plan, is lit by a single small window. Inside is a large statue of Champa, with serene expression, hands joined in the posture of teaching. The image, in the seated position, is installed high on the altar and there is a covered and enclosed opening in the ceiling to accommodate the upper part of the figure.

Jamyang, the *gönyer* or temple custodian, receives us. He possesses several life histories of the saints and is usually ready (in return for some grain) to read one of these works when, in the winter, his duties permit him. Year after year, Jamyang reads the life story of Milarepa. The women and youngsters who gather at the temple, in an enclosure protected from the wind, listen attentively to the story of the unhappy childhood of Milarepa. All that happened long ago, but it could happen again, tomorrow, in a nearby valley or even in the valley of Tarap.

At last we are on our way! In the bottom of the valley the fields have already been planted; they were sown in the beginning of the Third Month. Barley is the only cereal which can be cultivated at such an altitude (more than 4,000 meters), and to a large extent the survival of the local people depends on this crop. This year, however, barley was not sown on the higher terraces due to a shortage of water. The fields, laid out in terraces, are separated by dry stone walls raised to protect the crops against incursions by the livestock.

The yaks and sheep graze the slopes, gradually extending their range higher, as far up as there is growth of grass. The members of each family divide their time between activities relating to the house and the nearby fields, and their pastoral activities. Women perform the greatest number of tasks, in the valley attending to the weeding and the irrigation of the fields and in the pastures attending to the milking and the caring for the herds.

About one hundred meters above the valley floor and the populated area, the condition of the vegetation changes abruptly. Here the land is not so heavily grazed, and wildflowers are abundant: artemisia, asters (called "sheep's eye"), potentillas, primulas.

At the end of an hour's walk, we reach the first pasture, with its enclosures of dry stone walls and its circles of large rocks which surround the tent sites. Sharing Drong (the pasture of Sharing) belongs to the households of Kagar. The pasture is close to a temple whose name it bears. The white walls of the temple stand out sharply on a natural foundation of rock. Higher up the slope are the houses of Traglung, the residences of the religious ones who look after the temple of Sharing.

Pema Puti, helped by two of her sons, Chögya and Nyima Tenzin, is looking after the animals of three households of Kagar. She is pregnant and, in spite of her advanced condition (she will deliver in another month at the pasture), still undertakes all the work in the camp, which consists of milking twelve *dri* and about twenty she-goats and ewes. She knows our plan and wants to know more about the itinerary; particularly, the temples that we will visit. At her invitation, we seat ourselves under the tent, to the right of the hearth, the place of honor. She offers us creamy clotted milk and *tsampa*, and then makes us buckwheat bread.

Before leaving Pema Puti's tent, Karma goes over carefully, for the last time, the things he is carrying. Hooked to his belt are a sling, a little dagger with a silver handle in a finely engraved sheath, a punch, some awls, some needles in the copper shell of a cartridge; placed inside his *chuba*, on level with the belt, in a "pocket" called *ambag*, he has a tea bowl made of a rhododendron burl, a little spindle to twist yarn, some wool, some pieces of yak hide to repair the soles of his boots, a small sack of dried cheese, and a prayer wheel. He asks Pema Puti for a little yak hair for making thread. Then he carefully examines the contents of his reliquary, *jilab tagsa*, "the box of blessings." The reliquary's cover of embossed silver bears the eight auspicious symbols of happiness around a central opening which is shaped like a lotus petal. The copper box itself contains a little image of Green Drolma (Sanskrit, Tara); a paper on which the hand impressions of the Jowo statue of Lhasa[3] are printed, another which depicts the *gompa* of Chöku, situated on the pilgrim's trail around the sacred Kang Tisé; a piece of the garment and some hairs of the late Venerable Lama of Shang; some medical pills given by the same lama; a piece of *togchag*, "iron fallen from the heavens," which protects against calamities; and finally the turquoise given by Kagar Rinpoché.

Karma throws three pinches of *tsampa* as an offering into the hearth, settles his pack by making it seesaw from one shoulder to the other, and we set off.

Having crossed the stream, we look at the tent that we have just left. Pema Puti is standing by the tent, her arms hanging down alongside her body, impassive. She stands there a long time. The trail, much marked by passing herds, follows the stream, between tamarisks and dwarf willows.

Trangdrug
the Magician

The heron has long legs but his wings are not strong;
The antelope has long horns but they never touch the stars in the sky.

As we had anticipated, we are able to make good progress in the morning. The trail crosses over several pastures and includes difficult sections over boulders and I am reminded of a proverb often quoted by the people of Tarap: "In the day, it is hot three times and cold three times. In life, one is unhappy three times and happy three times."

In the northwest of Nepal, suspended in the high chain of Muligangs (which we of the West call the Dhaulagiri Massif), the pastures stand out in the grand but arid landscape.

However, it is not the vast uninhabited spaces that we stop to admire, it is a yak, a magnificent white yak, and Karma is wondering to whom it belongs.

As he watches the animal, Karma alludes, as he so often does, to the *lha*, the *tsen* and the *lu*, divinities which are associated respectively with the heavens, the intermediate space, and the underground—that is, the three "levels" of the world. This is actually a simple representation of a complex cosmology, in which the role of the Buddha is somewhat more difficult to comprehend.

Karma, looking at the yak, informs me that a yak which is entirely white, with white horns, is associated with the *lha;* while a yak with a black coat and black horns is associated with the Protector Gompo[4]; the yak with a brown coat and white forehead is associated with the *tsen;* and the yak with a blue coat and white hocks is associated with the *lu.*

Leaving the animal to its ruminating, we continue our trek and at the end of two hours of climbing, we make our first halt. The first portion of the day's march is always rather long; the successive stages, aided by fatigue, seem shorter and shorter, and the resting halts seem to get longer up to the moment of pitching camp. It is in the course of the first halt that Karma tells a story of yaks:

> In the Changtang, an old woman had only a single *dri* which bore the name of Yang-gam, "Box of good augury." Each year, the old woman hoped for a calf, but the *dri* remained sterile. Finally, she decided to slaughter it and buy another.
>
> "Old woman, if you kill me, you will die also! If one cuts the roots of a tree, it dies," the *dri* declared.
>
> The old woman then tried to sell the animal, but had no success. Vexed, the old woman gave the *dri* to a rich breeder, the owner of a large herd of yaks. The *dri* thought, "The old woman has given me to a rich *drogpa*, how is she going to feed herself?" The *dri* Yang-gam left the *drogpa's* herd, climbed toward the upper part of the valley, and after a very long walk, approached the tent of the old woman. She rubbed her head against a stay which vibrated with a sound, *"urting-urting."* The old woman came out and saw the *dri.* Happy indeed, she caressed her head and her ears. The *dri* remained in the pasture, sometimes on the valley floor, sometimes on the slopes where she met a yak with white and black coat, and they mated.
>
> The *dri* delivered two little ones, a male and a female. The old woman, fearing thieves, stayed day and night near the newborns and, although hungry, she left all the milk for the young calves. The young ones thrived. At the end

of a month, they appeared to be a year old, at one year
they appeared three years old and the female began to
calve, producing numerous descendants, a source of
wealth for the old woman.

So, when one speaks of a productive *dri*, it is said to be
the descendant of *Dri Lhamdri samu yang-gam.*

We resume our climb to the Khyung-la; the approach to the
pass is very steep, and, on this first day of the trek, the stops to
catch our breath are frequent. The storm which breaks almost
every afternoon in the spring catches us during our climb.

The Khyung-la is the first pass that we cross on our pilgrimage and we place a white stone, picked up lower down the
slope, on the *labtsé* (cairn) that marks the pass. To one of the
many poles already carrying numerous prayer flags, Karma
attaches one we have brought with us, a representation of the
horse carrying the Triple Jewel.[5]

The bird Khyung,[6] after whom this pass is named, is frequently represented in Tibetan paintings and is always depicted
full face, with rotund body and powerful wings. It is said to eat
jewels and to attack demons. *Zi*-beads, cylindrical banded ag-
ates which are worn around the neck by Tibetans, are thought
to be its solidified dung.

Karma remembers a story he had heard at Kagar from the
lips of Lama Rinpoché, and tells it to us:

> A very long time ago the bird Khyung laid an egg which
> a dragon took under its wings, and one day a very small
> man, the height of a cubit, emerged from the egg! This
> little man[7] flew away on the back of the dragon, who
> placed him near the White Lioness of the Glaciers, at the
> top of a high peak. The White Lioness suckled the little
> man with her own milk. A hunter made his way to the cave
> of the lioness and saw the little man, then eight years old.
> "Who are you?" the hunter asked. "Where do you come
> from? What is your lineage?"
> The child related his story. The hunter took him away
> and brought him up. This child became the chieftain of a

land which was given the name of Khyung-lung, "the land of the bird Khyung."

The little man had three hundred and sixty faithful servants who were loyal to him and who all became *po-lha* (ancestor gods) when they died. But he did not have any descendants.

Karma continues:

Many years later, a woman was weaving some cloth, the weather was clear, not a cloud in the sky, when suddenly a large hailstone fell near her, and as the woman was thirsty, she ate it. She later gave birth to a child who was given the name Shangtarpig. Shangtarpig met a giant with nine heads who became his *po-lha*, and helped him to establish himself in the valley. He became chieftain of the area and went on to establish himself at Nyi-Shang, east of Kang Tisé.

Shangtarpig took a girl from Dolpo for his wife, by whom he had two sons, Tashi Palden and Namka. Tashi Palden had numerous descendants. Namka went off to Sikkim.

One day Shangtarpig said to his wife: "I will die in twenty-one days."

"How can you know so precisely the day of your death?" she asked. "You are neither lama nor the incarnation of a holy man."

Nevertheless, on the day he said, Shangtarpig died in the position of meditation.

Karma began to give, in a jumble, fragments of the origins of the lineages of Western Tibet. The name of the clan founded by Shangtarpig was *Karma-mindrug* (the Pleiades), on account of his heavenly origin.[8]

In such an inhospitable environment, where people cannot find comfort and rocks are repeatedly shattered due to the extreme temperatures, one can readily imagine such fantastic animals as the bird Khyung and the Lioness of the Glaciers!

We have been delayed and are not able to reach the traditional campsite on the trail between Tarap and Shey. The sun begins to set, and we are forced to spend the night out under the stars on the north slope of the pass.

The sun disappears. It begins to be cold and damp. To feed a fire we have only twigs, some dried yak dung, and a few twigs of dwarf rhododendron which Norbu cuts nearby. We mix our *tsampa* with barely tepid tea and a little butter.

Karma removes one of his *lhamdrog* (boot garter strings), folds it over once, and then folds the already folded mass again. He then locates the two ends of the cord and pulls them out of the folded mass—the "knot" comes apart, it does not tangle. "It is a good sign," he says to me, interpreting this ritual which is a form of divination.

We all stretch out on one side of the fire, huddling closely together for warmth. Norbu, thinking about the three of us, quotes the folk-saying, "Three men will only travel together if they are tied by friendship and have a common goal."

Karma begins speaking in a voice which is barely audible:

> In the land of Tö, the king had a son; in the land of Mé, the minister had a son; and in the land of Par, a poor woman had a son. She was so poor that her child was always naked and his skin became blue, from which came his name: Trangdrug Ngöntrag, "the beggar's child with blue blood."
>
> The three children, united in friendship, often played *taka* (knuckle-bones) together. Trangdrug was constantly the winner. The minister was outraged and went to plead with the king:
>
> "King of the land of Tö: Trangdrug, the son of a beggar, wins all the time. Tomorrow, he may win our kingdom. It is necessary to expel him."
>
> The king was easily convinced and expelled first the mother, then the child. But Trangdrug's two playmates resolved to leave with him.
>
> After a long trek, the three children fell asleep, exhausted, at the summit of a pass, beside a *labtsé*. Before sleeping, however, Trangdrug laid his knuckle-bones out on the trail, the "horse" side upwards.[9]

The king and the minister sent their best horsemen in pursuit of the children. Awakened by the sound of the horses, Trangdrug pronounced the magical words "Haa," followed by "Huu," transforming the knuckle-bones into colorful horsemen who blocked the way. The king's army took fright and turned back.

The children, continuing on their way, arrived at the base of a cliff and, after having drunk pure, sacred water, fell asleep. But Trangdrug stayed awake.

In a hollow on the cliff there was an owl's nest. The male arrived, calling, "I have something to eat and something to drink. The king's mule is dead and I have brought some liver and lung."

The female, quite pleased, said, "Shug shug shug."

Trangdrug understood these words of the owl.

The fledgling asked, "What is there to eat today?" The mother replied, "There are lots of tasty bits. Among them, liver and lung of mule have magical powers: if one eats of them, one obtains everything; only don't eat too much." And she put some of the meat on the edge of the nest.

The next day, the owl came back to the nest and said, "Today the king has to perform a ritual for finding his son. We must go there and bring back some *torma*."

Trangdrug, taking advantage of the owls' absence, climbed up to the nest. He took some of the liver, ate a part, and saved the rest. He also found a blue and white turquoise in the shape of a goat's liver, and this he brought away. Trangdrug crushed the turquoise, making it into powder.

The children set out again. After a little while they saw, rising above a pasture, the smoke from an encampment. A shepherdess was cooking some mutton; she gave a piece to each of the boys, and Trangdrug mixed a little of the turquoise powder with the meat. He also asked for the right shoulder blade of the sheep.

After having thanked the shepherdess they went on, and arrived in a rich and prosperous land. In the evening, Trangdrug made a divination with the shoulder blade, putting it in the fire.[10] He invoked his *yidam*. "The king's son, where must he go? The minister's son, where must he go?" he asked.

The response came: "The king's son will become the son-in-law of a powerful king. The minister's son will become the son-in-law of a powerful minister."

The next day the three friends set out and arrived at a bridge. A *towo* (a stack of three stones) and a guard blocked their way. On the other side of the river, there was a large house which resembled a palace.

The guard spoke: "Do not cross over this bridge! You will be entering the realm of a powerful king."

"If there is a bridge on the river, but there is no right of passage, then what is the use of the bridge?" replied Trangdrug, who then crossed over, followed by his two friends.

At the door to the palace, a guard told them, "It is forbidden to enter into the court."

"If there is a door at the entrance of the palace, what use can it serve if one cannot enter or leave through it?" asked Trangdrug. And the three friends went through the door and into the court. The king, seated on his throne of gold, saw the children arrive and showed his astonishment:

"I have posted a guard at the bridge and another in front of the door; how can it be that these children have been able to get past these obstacles? Who are you and where do you come from?" demanded the king.

"The sky is my father, the earth is my mother," said Trangdrug. "My friend here is the son of a king; my other friend is a minister's son. Give us a task to accomplish, like looking after yaks, horses, or sheep; and we will fulfill it with dedication."

They stayed the night and the king made them work one day, then he told them:

"I am a powerful king and no one has ever managed to enter my kingdom without my permission; but, as my only child is a daughter, I will give her to a king's son, a child of noble birth."

Trangdrug's friend wanted to refuse, but Trangdrug convinced him to stay and to marry the princess. The king's son was wise and good because he had eaten some of the turquoise powder, which had great power.

Trangdrug made a prayer and collected some flowers. He gave some to his friend, the king's son: "The flowers are similar to the soul; as long as they bloom, the soul and the body are in good health; if a flower withers, the body suffers."

On the occasion of the marriage of his daughter, the king arranged a big feast which lasted seven days, with much celebrating, horse races, archery competitions, and other games which encourage good fortune. Then, Trangdrug and the minister's son prepared to set out again, to go far away.

The king saw the flowers left by Trangdrug and asked his new son-in-law: "What are these three flowers?"

"The white flower represents the *lha*; the red flower represents the *tsen*; the blue flower represents the *lu*."

Trangdrug and his friend, the minister's son, left. They came to a bridge where a *towo* rose up to the sky. They said to the guard at the bridge and to the guard at the door of the palace who warned them against proceeding: "What is the use of a bridge if one cannot pass over it? What is the use of a door if one cannot pass through it?" They then entered the palace of the powerful minister.

"Who are you?" the minister demanded.

"The sky is my father, the earth is my mother. My companion is the son of the minister of the land of Mé."

Hearing these words, the powerful minister gave his daughter to the son of the minister of Mé, who did not want to stay; however, Trangdrug persuaded him to remain and handed over to him three flowers, as he had done for the king's son.

There was rejoicing for seven days, with horse-racing, archery, and all; then Trangdrug, alone, set out on his way.

He arrived in a place where some children were quarrelling with each other. One had a hat, another a whip, the third a saddle bag. Trangdrug demanded: "What are you beating each other for?"

"We each have a possession of great power—if I tap three times on the ground with my whip, I can go anywhere I want to," said the first child.

"If I wear this hat, I become invisible," said the second.

The third said, "When I put my hand into this saddle bag, if I make a wish for food, I find raw sugar, sugar candy, butter; this is the bag *gangde shamar yag* ('giving a lot of good meat and butter')."

"Which of these is the most powerful object? This is the reason for our dispute," said all three.

Trangdrug reflected, and said, "Don't dispute. I have a method by which you can settle everything. Run a race; the first to arrive has the most powerful object. Run now, I will watch your things." Trangdrug took the bag and the whip in his hands and, not knowing what to do with the hat, he instinctively put it on his head without being aware that he was becoming invisible!

The three children ran the race, then returned to their starting place, but they could not find Trangdrug! They searched for a long time and in the end they went away. Trangdrug, for his part, was tired out from waiting. He took off the hat and didn't see anyone. He thought: "Those children have told me stories," and in order to see for himself, he made a wish: "May there be tea, may there be butter." He plunged his hand into the bag and immediately got a large amount of tea and butter!

"The children have indeed told the truth. These things have great magic power. How am I to return these precious objects to them?" And Trangdrug set out to search the world for the children.

Trangdrug walked a long time. One day he arrived near an encampment. He put on the hat that makes one invisible, in order to better study the people and the tents. And then he saw a beautiful girl. Raising his hat, he asked, "Which encampment is this? And to which clan does it belong?"

"These are tents of the *drogpa* of the heights. What is your name?" she replied.

"I am called Chachatiwa,[11] and I am looking for a shelter for the night," he said.

"Ask for hospitality from my mother who is busy milking the goats," the girl told him.

The mother said, "Stay under our tent; there is only my daughter and I, but what is your name?"

"Chochichi,"[12] replied Trangdrug.

At nightfall, the mother made a fire, prepared the tea, and got ready to sleep. Trangdrug put the hat in one side of the bag, the whip in the other. Then, with the bag as a pillow, he lay down at the middle of the tent between the mother and the girl, who slept at a lower level. It began to rain, and Trangdrug took advantage of this to pass quietly to the lower part of the tent, to the place where the girl was, and began to caress her. In surprise, she cried, "Mother, Mother, it's raining[13]; I can't sleep!"

"Since it rains, get close to make love."[14] The girl obeyed her mother and Trangdrug made love with her all night, and for the next seven nights also. On the eighth day, Trangdrug noticed that the white flower which he had kept was wilting.

"I must leave; one of my friends is in danger, but I will come again, very soon," said Trangdrug.

He hit the ground with the whip three times: "Let me be at the king's palace."

Arriving at the palace, Trangdrug put the magic hat on his head, and, invisible, went in looking for his friend.

That night, he saw a stranger arrive who went to the bed of the king's daughter. Trangdrug thought: "Where is my friend?" Invisible, he followed the girl, who went to a secluded room of the palace and he discovered his friend there, locked in. Trangdrug went close to him.

"Oh! You are here," said the king's son as Trangdrug took off the hat that had made him invisible.

"What has happened? Are you unhappy?" asked Trangdrug.

"At the beginning, everything went well, but now, I am deprived of everything. The king has taken a second son-in-law who has all the powers," said his friend.

"This man must be killed, and we must leave," said Trangdrug.

He and his friend stayed together for seven days, eating at their pleasure, thanks to the magic bag. They ate well and drank sweet beer. Each time the daughter came, Trangdrug would put on his hat. Invisible, he would beat the second husband who, covered with wounds of an unknown origin, was between life and death.

The king made many religious rituals to cure his second son-in-law, but in vain. Finally he heard mention of a lama of great power, a *togden* (this was Trangdrug in disguise), and had him summoned. On being consulted, Trangdrug interpreted a divination: "O king," he said, appearing to be frightened, "I have never made such a divination, and I do not dare reveal the interpretation to you."

The king reassured the *togden*: "I will give you whatever you want—if necessary, even my treasures—but tell me the cause of my son-in-law's sickness."

"O king, I do not dare to tell you! Permit me to live after you have heard me interpret the divination! Your first son-in-law is the son of a deity. If you do not turn out the second son-in-law, you both are going to die soon." Later, Trangdrug recounted these events to his friend. In the meantime, the king thought, "This *togden* is wrong— I will not torment my son-in-law." The king then sent for his minister and assembled his subjects in order to reveal the meaning of the divination, and said to them: "What must I do? The divination commands the removal of the second son-in-law, the first being the son of a deity. I myself will die if I do not carry out this verdict."

Then the minister proposed that the king, in order to guard the lives of both his sons-in-law, construct two palaces: the king's daughter would then go from one to the other without either son-in-law being aware of this strategy. The king agreed to follow this advice.

Trangdrug, invisible, had heard everything. He beat the son-in-law, then also the king, for one whole night. The king, covered with wounds, decided to turn out the second son-in-law and he recovered instantaneously. The daughter, however, decided to leave with the banished son-in-law. Once again, Trangdrug surprised them. He went by a group of *chörten*, took a little white dust from the white *chörten* and a little black dust from the black *chörten*.[15] He then scattered the black dust all around the daughter of the king and the second son-in-law, who both became fixed to the ground.

The king, not knowing what to do to free them, again appealed to the *togden*. "I offer you a part of my treasure if you can free these two beings."

"O king! I do not want anything, but I also do not want to be killed if I reveal the meaning of my divination to you. You did not wish to hear me the first time. To save your life and that of your daughter, the second son-in-law must be turned out. Only this way will you and your kingdom be saved."

The second son-in-law was finally banished and Trangdrug's friend found happiness again.

Trangdrug then saw that the blue flower was beginning to wither. Invisible, he set out for the land of the powerful minister where he found his second friend suffering in the same way. Thanks to the hat that makes one invisible, he could help his friend to find power and happiness again. So, he was well served by the whip that transports one far away, the little hat that makes one invisible, and the saddle bag *gangde shamar yag* that grants all desires.

Having helped his two friends, and they now being reestablished with their rights, Trangdrug thought of his old mother. He struck three blows with the magic whip and was immediately near her. She was extremely happy, and Trangdrug, powerful with his magic bag, served up a large amount of excellent food.

"Have you been stealing?" his mother wanted to know. Trangdrug related his long adventure: the flight with his two friends; the accidental meeting with the three children quarrelling on the subject of the value of their magic objects. Then his mother gave him the answer which the children had sought: "The best thing is the magic bag; the least good is the hat; and in between them is the whip."

Trangdrug returned afterwards to the encampment of the girl where he stayed for one year, one month and one day, before again going to meet his two friends. All three then decided to go back to their native place. In time they all arrived at their parental homes. The old king, the old minister and the old lady were all happy to see their children.

Trangdrug then returned to the *drogpa* encampment and decided to build a house. In the night, he made an offering, pronouncing the magical words "Haa" and "Huu," and in the morning there appeared a fine three-story house in the plain. He invited his two friends and their fathers-in-law, who had become very cordial now with their sons-in-law.

Trangdrug then resumed the appearance of the *togden*. Recognizing him, the king and the minister treated him with deference.

In his private chapel, Trangdrug had hung up the hat, the whip and the saddle bag on the wall. The king and the minister were unable to understand what good these three things could serve. The king decided to put the question to Trangdrug, to which Trangdrug gave this reply: "These three things are responsible for my wealth."

The king, on returning to his palace, had a hat, a whip and a saddle bag put on the wall, and asked Trangdrug the *togden* to consecrate them, hoping thus to acquire a similar fortune himself.

Here the story stops. Karma adds, as if for himself, "The three friends were linked by an oath, as the proverb says: 'Three men, a single soul.'"

Before falling asleep, Norbu puts several pinches of *tsampa* on the embers as an offering to the *sadag*, divinities of the earth, for favorable weather. Karma again makes a divination, this time with his sling. He carefully folds up the sling and then locates and catches the two ends, pulls on them, and observes the result of the unfolding. It is a propitiatory rite for our journey. He watches the night a long time, his rosary in his hand.

The Quest of the Flower Utumwara

Wet wood can still burn;
Dry stones will never burn.

None of us is able to get much sleep; the night is just too cold and too damp. There is little we can do but wait for morning. We then stretch out in the sunshine to get warm before returning to the trail to Shey. Norbu compares us to three beggars: "We only lack a two-stringed fiddle and the skill to snare marmots!" This causes Karma to speak up:

> Once upon a time, there were three beggars: one was bald and scratched his head; another had eye trouble and rubbed his eyes all the time; the third had mange and was always rubbing the skin of his hands and arms. Troubled by all this scratching, they made a vow to stop, but it was very difficult.
>
> One day they were stretched out along the edge of the road and the hot summer sunshine again inflamed their itches. The one who had trouble with his eyes said to his companions: "I am going to tell you a story. Long, long ago, my grandfather had a ram with immense horns..." and he made a gesture to illustrate, passing his hands

before his eyes and rubbing them, as he pantomimed horns
with his extended fingers.

The man with the mange then said: "I am going to tell
you a story: my father was an archer so skilled that he
was able to draw the bow as well with the left hand as
with the right hand," and he illustrated this by scratching
himself energetically under the arms.

"Your two stories have truly made an impression in my
mind," said the third beggar, vigorously scratching his bald
head.

This story, or rather the antics of the storyteller, causes us to
stop and laugh.

A little beyond the Khyung-la, near where we spent the night,
we come to a crossing of trails. The trail that comes from the
north, along the side of the mountain, is actually a series
of trails, many of which are deeply furrowed and filled with
very loose sand, heavily churned by the hooves of yaks, and
on both sides the ground is without vegetation. The path continues toward the west, in the direction of Reng and of the lake
of Tso, whose water is "poisoned by water from the heart of a
demoness."

A large caravan of pack-goats and yaks is climbing up from
the east, from Nangkhong, and meets us. It is headed toward
the valley of Reng and further to Western Nepal, "the land of
rice and spices." Two men drive the animals, one whistling and
making the goats move before him, the second, often snapping
his sling, walks behind the yaks which are even more unman-
ageable than the goats. Seeing us, both men sit down and await
our arrival. We join them and share a buckwheat cake and a
few chillies.

Karma examines the sling, *urtu*, and says to me: "The sling is
the weapon of choice. There are many kinds of slings; the sling
with 'nine eyes' has the power of the Protective Deities against
all enemies; the sling with braided strings of eight colors is used
by girls; the sling with white braided strings is for children; the
sling with black and white braided strings is used by yak-men;

the sling made of dog hair has a special power—a stone thrown from this sling does not break the bones of the animal it was aimed at."

Fortified by our snack, we return to the trail on a slope of rubble and schist debris. In the middle of the afternoon, we reach the Mugchung-la. A *labtsé* guards the pass. Scattered around the pass are piles of stones and numerous *khangpa*, the little stone "houses" which pilgrims erect while making a wish to live here in the next life.

It takes another two hours to reach the group of temples and houses that is Shey, situated at the confluence of two streams.

Shey is a complex of buildings and walls fitted with prayer wheels and piles of stones engraved with religious verses. The principal temple, in earlier times, belonged to the Kagyupa order; its altar is adorned with a very beautiful bronze image of Dorjechang.[16] At this time, the officiating monks are in Namgung, their winter residence, working in the fields. A monk from Tarap, Pemba of the house of Shönzang, offers us hospitality in a little room that he occupies over one of the temples.

Some tea, then a soup of nettles and some *tsampa* fill us up. Karma, perhaps reminded of the theme of friends united by an oath, relates this story:

> In the land of Tö, the king's son, the minister's son, the rich trader's son and the beggar's son were all bound by ties of friendship. They decided to make a tour of the land of Tö, and the king gave his son three gold coins.
>
> One day, the friends arrived in a village of stonecutters. The king's son asked the villagers: "How do the people of this village earn their livelihood? What crafts and skills are practiced here?"
>
> "Stone is cut here," the people replied.
>
> The king's son then said to the trader's son: "Stay here and learn the craft of the stonecutter." And he gave a gold

coin to the master quarry-man to pay for teaching his craft to the boy. The others went on and arrived at a village of blacksmiths.

"What craft is practiced here?" asked the king's son. "Iron is worked here, and iron palaces are built," was the answer. The king's son asked the beggar's son to learn the craft of forging iron, and to compensate for this, he gave a gold coin to the master of the forge.

The two remaining friends left and in time arrived in the land of the masters of divination.

"What does one learn in this place?"

"We practice astrological calculations and divinations," was the reply. The minister's son stayed to learn calculation and divination and the master who was to teach him received a gold coin.

"When each of you three have learned your craft we will meet together again," said the king's son.

The king's son then arrived alone at the edge of a large lake where stood the palace of a demon, just beside a garden filled with flowers.

In the palace there were two yak tails which had special powers; one was the tail of a white yak and one the tail of a black yak. When touched with the black tail, one falls into a deep sleep, resembling death; then only a touch with the white tail can bring back life. These objects belonged to the demon and were used to capture young men and to keep them prisoner.

In the garden a young woman of exceptional beauty was asleep and the king's son instantly fell in love with her. Gazing at her, he said to himself: "This girl is so beautiful she can only be a deity." He saw the two yak tails and brushed the girl with the white tail. She awoke then and he asked her many questions, and discovered that there were many young men living in the palace whom the girl would awake at night with the white tail, and put to sleep at dawn with the black tail. The king's son found them asleep and shook the white tail over them.

"What are you all doing here?"

"We are on a search for a marvelous flower, Utumwara, which resembles a jewel and is unique in the world. It is to be found in the center of the lake. But, arriving at the shore, we were captured by a demon and imprisoned. With the flower Utumwara, one can restore life to a loved one, give sight to the blind and do other marvelous things."

"Have you found this flower?" asked the king's son.

"No," was the reply.

"Would you not like to stay to look for it?"

"No," was the reply.

The king's son asked, "How can one come to possess the marvelous flower if it is at the unreachable center of the evil lake?"

"If you kill the demon's daughter, the lake will dry up and the flower will be accessible."

And the young men, now freed, went away.

In the evening the girl found only the king's son, the other young men having departed. Furious, she touched him with the black tail. He was immediately put to sleep. At nightfall he was given a meal, and this went on for some years.

One day, the minister's son, who had been instructed in the art of divination, thought to himself: "I would like to find out where my friend, the king's son, is." He then performed a divination ritual and learned that the king's son was in trouble, his body having become like a corpse. The minister's son then went to the village of iron workers to meet his friend who was there.

"The king's son, our friend, is in difficulty; this I have learned by divination," he told the master of the forge.

The master of the forge climbed a high iron tower which commanded a view of the entire world. He saw the king's son asleep on the other side of a large lake. The minister's son and the trader's son went off to find their friend, the beggar's son, to tell him the bad news.

The three friends then set out. They arrived on the bank of the lake and found their friend asleep. Nothing could wake him! The minister's son, by divination, asked if the king's son was dead: "The white tail will bring him back to life," was the reply. He then shook the white tail and the king's son awoke.

The king's son related his adventures and then said: "There is a rare flower here which is at the center of the lake, but to obtain it, the demon's daughter has to be killed. Only if this girl is killed will the lake dry up and we be able to reach the flower. But we must learn how to distinguish the demon's daughter from all the other girls that are gathered here."

A divination was made which advised that the girl called Yujum Drolma was to be killed.

"Which one carries this name?" the four friends asked.

"This girl passes the day in the garden and at night returns to the center of the lake."

"How is the girl to be killed?"

"If one is able to cut the stem of the flower that supports the throne, one kills the girl."

"What is the appearance of the flower?"

"The marvelous flower has three petals, two in the ears of the girl, the third is under her throne surrounded by water."

The beggar's son then made an iron bridge reaching to the center of the lake.

That night, the king's son went to the center of the lake. The girl spoke to him: "No man has ever come here; if the demon learns about it he will kill you."

"I have come to take you and the marvelous flower!"

"If you take me away, the lake will disappear and the demon will be utterly destroyed! This is because I am the flower Utumwara!"

The king's son tried to cut the stem, which was as hard as rock. He asked the girl: "How is the flower Utumwara to be obtained?"

The girl replied: "I am the flower Utumwara! To take me away is to destroy the palace of the demon. If this is to be, then listen: On my demon-father's head is a hat, and at the top of this hat there is a jewel, *norbu chushel*. Only with this jewel can the stem of the flower Utumwara be cut."

The king's son then asked: "How is this jewel to be obtained?"

The minister's son then performed a divination and the response was: "The entrance of the palace is guarded by tigers and leopards; the demon can be killed only with a quarry-man's hammer."

The beggar's son then hit the demon with his heavy hammer on the nose and on the chest, killing him, and thus they got hold of the jewel *norbu chushel*.

Then the girl said: "Do not kill me or you will destroy the flower and the demon's palace."

The king's son again asked for the flower. The girl then gave him the petal from her right ear, and immediately she could no longer see from her right eye, and the lake emptied itself a little. The king's son himself detached the petal from the left ear. The girl became blind, and the lake dried up some more. Then the king's son struck the stem with the jewel *norbu chushel*, severing it and freeing the entire flower.

The four friends came back again into their country with the marvelous flower and the jewel *norbu chushel*.

The demon's daughter had said: "If the stem of the flower is broken, from each petal a girl will be born." Of the three girls born that day, one became the wife of the king's son; the second the wife of the minister's son; and the third the wife of the trader's son. The beggar's son retained the jewel *norbu chushel*, with which he created the most beautiful works of art. And the kingdom became prosperous.

Once Karma's story is over, we are able to look about the room where we have been received. It is rectangular, with a low ceiling, and it contains a hearth, an earthen stove with two openings. Above the hearth, a set of shelves hold cooking utensils. On each side of the room is a raised platform covered with cushions and antelope skins. These skins are said to discourage lice, which is an important advantage in a region where they abound.

The room is dimly lit by a small butter lamp; we are stretched out, too tired to sleep. But Karma is again ready to tell a story!

Long, long ago in Tibet, in the West lived the king Berakha, and in the East lived the king Garadrug. The people of the Middle did not have a chieftain and power there was periodically coveted by the two neighboring kings. But the men of the Middle wished to decide for themselves their own fate, as they thought that a king from a distant region was "like the cold which the wind brings when it blows over the ridge of a mountain."

The two kings insisted that the men of the Middle find themselves a chieftain. They said: "If you do not have a chief, you have no law." The men of the Middle, after discussing amongst themselves, decided to designate one of themselves as chieftain. The two kings were very disappointed not to have been chosen.

There was a courageous and wise man in the Middle, and it was he who had been chosen. He was given the name Gyalwo Kaga Yangdzi. The two neighboring kings then proposed a meeting to select the most intelligent chieftain and they chose the Middle as the place for this meeting.

The kings of the East and the West asked the king of the Middle: "Do you now have a law?"

The king of the Middle replied: "Earlier, there was no king in the Middle and yet there has always been a law:

On the earth there is a law for the grass,
In the water there is a law for the water,
Therefore there is a law."

The two kings gave some thought to this. "How can there be a law for the grass, how can there be a law for the water?" they asked.

The king of the Middle then said: "Earlier, there was no king in our country and now you ask me how then there could have been a law for the grass and a law for the water? Well! What can people do without grass from the pasture and without water to irrigate the fields? You have to agree that the most basic law is that which governs the use of grass and water."

The king of the East remained unconvinced, but the king of the West regretted having doubted the intelligence of the man from the Middle as he had to recognize his wisdom. The king of the East was furious and proposed a horse race with a view to getting even.

Preparations were made on the plain of the Middle. The king of the Middle cleverly sat very quickly on the center throne, obliging the two others to be seated, one at his right, the other at his left. Thus it was before him only that the offerings were placed.

The celebrations continued for seven days. Before departing, the king of the Middle said: "The king remains seated, unmoved; the field rat is seated, a little bent; the tiger stands with shoulders high."

The king of East did not understand the reference, but the king of the West recognized himself in that image, and said to the king of the Middle: "You are like the center between two extremes, like the heart in the middle of the chest." And the king of the West joined the service of the king of the Middle and became his wise minister.

Pemba has listened attentively, as have Norbu and I, to Karma and the stories he tells as we drink tea. Karma has revealed himself to be a master storyteller, dramatizing his narrations with gusto, adopting different intonations to suit the various characters and circumstances. Actually, Karma is happy telling stories; there may be merit to be gained by this telling.

Pemba then tells us about the various features of the *nékhor* of Shey mountain, our itinerary for the next day. The pilgrims' trail, with its sacred spots, winds around the mountain, which rises to more than 6,000 meters. Lama Trutob Sengé Yeshé, having come from Tibet, had "opened" this pilgrimage. He possessed a special power, which certain hermits have, of foreseeing future happenings, of visualizing sacred places, which they then reveal to those who seek their veneration. So it has been with the pilgrims' trail around the mountain of Shey. Pemba explains that Sengé Yeshé was a *togden*, "one who is realized." This title is given at the end of a seclusion which lasts three years, three months, and three days and whose last phase consists of a series of meditations on the theme of light, having as a focus a lamp, then the sunrise, and finally the full sun in all its brilliance. This first meditation, "the clear light," is followed by a meditation of three months in total darkness. This second retreat puts to the test the results of the meditations on light.

The Shepherd-princess

Wisdom cannot be washed away in a fast stream;
It cannot be destroyed by fire.

Pemba wakes us with his prayers. Seated cross-legged, wrapped
in a striped woolen blanket, he rocks backward and forward
gently as he recites the morning invocation.

We set off after having a bowl of tea with *tsampa* and per-
forming the ritual burning of juniper. Pemba accompanies us.
We reach the confluence of two fast-running streams and follow the stream which drives a series of prayer wheels. These
are constructed on the principle of the horizontal paddle-wheel.

The path crosses a little water course flowing out of the "lake
of milk," whose water is considered beneficial. Close by is the
sanctuary of the *Po-lha* of Shey. It is built of dry stone, cubic in
form, about a meter high, painted white and surmounted by a
pole adorned with many colorful prayer flags that Lama Sherab
Dampa of Shey, the officiating lama, replaces every year on the
fifth day of the Fifth Month. A trickle of water emerges from
beneath a rock; it is said to be "one of the sources of the holy
river Ganga." The entire path is marked out regularly by small piles
of white stones; and with each passing, pilgrims add to them.

After walking for about an hour we come to a huge rock capped with a large pile of stones. Here there is a place for prostration, marked by two large poles supporting numerous prayer flags. The path slants away toward the north and climbs between two vertical cliffs, framing Lha-lung, the "Valley of the *Lha* Divinities." The rocks here resemble images of Drolma, the Divine Savioress, and mantras are carved on them in immense letters. At this place pilgrims remove a little crumbling soil from the face of the cliff on the left and swallow it. This soil is considered to be medicinal as well as a blessing.

Pemba calls our attention to a section of the mountain to the right: half way up runs a band of dark-colored rock: "It is the road that leads to Hell," he says, and the water that flows from the base of the rocks is malevolent.

Nearby, there is a pile of white stones from which water also emerges. This is holy water; it has healing powers. Here pilgrims make a short stop and, mixing this water with flour, prepare a little *tsampa*.

We next arrive in a large natural amphitheater where there are numerous heaps of white stones, calcite, and the rocks are carved with sacred letters. On the right, a large solitary rock is considered to represent the palace of Drolma in her twenty-one manifestations. Here we make a ritual burning of juniper branches. Then, while intoning a prayer for rebirth in this holy place, we collect flat stones and construct our own "houses," called *khangpa*.

The trail climbs to a pass, dedicated to Drolma, which we reach by midday. From here we can see the Tibetan plateau to the north, and to the west the impressive mass of the Kanjiroba. The pass itself is a sanctuary and is dominated by a construction in cubic form which is adorned with stones carved with mantras, some poles with prayer flags, and many yak, ram, and stag horns. In former times, before the "opening" of the pilgrimage, only certain animals, such as jackals, and demons in human form inhabited this place, but Lama Trutob Sengé Yeshé, who pioneered the pilgrimage, drove them away.

Beside the *labtsé* is a small pit where people leave teeth, hair
and human bones, as one prefers not to leave these items where
demons can take possession of them and then harm their own-
ers. Close by is a rock, a natural representation of Drolma, and
pilgrims cover it with butter. It is good to rest here, in order to
be inspired by Drolma, and Pemba tells us that pious people
sleeping here see Drolma in their dreams, who tells them their
future.

Here some other pilgrims join us, and we become some ten
listeners gathered around Karma as he describes Drolma in one
of her incarnations:

> A long time ago, there lived a king in Shar-ling, the
> country of the East, and a king in Nub-ling, the country of
> the West. The king of the West had a single daughter, beau-
> tiful and virtuous, an incarnation of Drolma. She lived in
> her father's palace and showed herself to her subjects at
> the time of each full moon, a lotus flower in hand.[17] Her
> beauty was known to all.
>
> One day, a trader from the land of the East, having come
> to the West for business, saw the princess. On returning to
> his country, the trader came to know that his own king
> wished to get his son married, but the son was not able to
> find a princess according to his taste. The trader then said
> to the king's son: "In the country of the West lives a prin-
> cess, daughter of a powerful king; she is an incarnation of
> Drolma."
>
> The king's son sent the trader with a letter for the prin-
> cess. Arriving in the land of the princess, the trader lodged
> with an old woman who gave him advice on how to ap-
> proach the princess. However, on the next day of the full
> moon so many people had assembled that he was not able
> to hand over the letter, yet he succeeded in slipping it into
> the princess's boot.
>
> In the evening, the princess, pulling off her boots, saw
> the letter and read it: "This message comes from the prince
> of the country of the East. If you are beautiful, listen! I am

powerful and skilled with weapons. Perhaps we could join together? If this pleases you, entrust your response to the carrier of this message."

"Who has been able to slip this message into my boot?" the princess asked herself. Her faithful servant made some enquiries and identified the trader, who explained the prince's purpose.

The princess then handed the trader a hand-sized piece of yellow silk. "Give it to the prince," she said. "If this piece of silk fits the window of his room, I will be his wife. But if it is either too large or too small, this will not happen."

The trader reported his experiences and gave the silk to the prince, who discovered that it fitted his window perfectly. "Happy omen!" he thought.

The prince asked the trader to accompany him to the country of the West. "No soldiers, no servants," he said, "for my father the king perhaps will not accept this marriage. Let us go alone with only our two excellent horses."

As soon as they arrived, the old woman gave the prince this advice: "To meet the princess, you must enter the palace at night. But pay attention! The palace is guarded by ferocious dogs. You must take some meat to distract the dogs and make your entry into the princess's house when the night is darkest."

This, then, is what the prince did. But as he had to wait until midnight, he grew drowsy and dozed near a large prayer-wheel. The princess saw him and placed some fruit beside him. Early the next morning, the prince awoke and saw the fruit, which he took with him, thinking that it could be a gift from the princess. He vowed to come back the next night.

The next night the prince again entered the palace and again he fell asleep as he waited.

The prince could not think how to keep himself awake. The trader advised him to cut himself with a knife and, when in the palace, to dress the wound with a special red

powder that he would give him, which was, unknown to the prince, red chilli powder! The prince then left with meat for the dogs, entered the palace and as his wound caused him to suffer, he remained completely awake. At midnight, he saw the princess, dazzling with beauty. He told her that the piece of silk was exactly the size of his window. They then passed the night together.

"Tomorrow," she said, "is the day of the full moon. I have to present myself to my people. But now that I am no longer pure, the flower of the lotus has faded. We must leave quickly, and go far from our two countries."

Mounting the two fine horses, they crossed India and arrived in a Muslim country. Soon they had exhausted all their resources, so the princess asked the prince to buy yellow silk fabric and some thread of the five ritual colors—yellow, green, red, white and blue. She then embroidered a beautiful image of Drolma on the yellow fabric.

"Go and sell this embroidery, but do not reply to any questions that are put to you," she told the prince. She also gave him a magic dagger. And she stayed behind, hidden in a cave.

The prince went straightaway to find a wealthy Muslim trader and offered him the embroidery. The trader, full of praise for the embroidery, put a thousand questions to him on its origin.

"I am the son of the king of the East," admitted the prince, who went on to relate the story of his life. The trader then offered him some fruit that put him to sleep. He stole the magic dagger, went into the cave and captured the princess, whom he took into his service.

Then the trader turned out the prince, who, dressed in rags, wandered through the country. To earn a living, he sewed women's clothing. In the course of his wanderings, he eventually returned to the trader's city, and one day the princess noticed him as he was embroidering a motif. She told her servant to call the poor man. The prince did not recognize her, but she told him:

"I am your wife, the princess of the country of the West; by your fault and your boasting, I have lost you and am now in the hands of the trader. Here is some money. Go and buy two fine horses, tie them up tonight at the foot of the wall, near the window, and we will escape together."

The prince bought two fast horses and excellent saddles. At nightfall, he tied the horses under the window, but then he fell asleep. Two thieves came up and took hold of the horses. At the same moment, the princess jumped onto one of the horses, thinking that the horseman was the prince. At daybreak, the thieves were surprised to find, behind, a beautiful princess covered with precious jewelry.

Each of the two robbers wanted her for his wife. The princess, taking advantage of their disagreement, proposed the following bargain to them: "Make a bow and an arrow. I will then shoot the arrow and the one who brings it back will marry me; the other one will have my jewelry."

While the two thieves fashioned the bow, the princess made a prayer so that the arrow would fly as far as possible. The arrow went over a high pass; the thieves immediately left for the search, and the princess took advantage of their departure to flee, disguising herself as a man.

In a distant country, still disguised as a man, she settled down, becoming a shepherd in the service of the king of the land, and, as she was an incarnation of Drolma, the herd increased to the point that the king put her in charge of his horses.

Thus three years passed while the princess kept busy with the king's horses, which prospered marvelously. Very satisfied, the king promoted the shepherd-princess to the rank of personal attendant and she advised him better than a wise minister would have done.

The king had only one child, a daughter, who refused all the suitors that were presented to her. The king decided to find her a husband, thinking to himself that his faithful attendant had all the required qualities! During a meeting with the princes of the neighboring lands, the king proposed: "The one who brings back nine right ears of deer will become my son-in-law," and he secretly encouraged his attendant to also leave for the hunt.

The princess-attendant did not know what to do and went to visit a saintly hermit she knew who was living as a recluse in the forest. Earlier, she had on occasion offered him milk from her ewes, and he expressed his surprise at not having seen her for such a long time.

"What has become of you? What brings you here?" he asked.

The princess explained to him the reason for her disguise, then the project of the king to see her become his son-in-law and inherit the kingdom! "But I am a woman and cannot be a prince!" she said.

"You will be a man," said the recluse, and because he was a master of rituals, he performed the necessary rites. The ceremony concluded, the princess acquired all the male attributes. Then the deer came in large numbers to the hermitage and the princess had only to cut off their right ears. The lama told her to set aside twenty-one, that is to say as many as the manifestations of Drolma.

On returning to the royal palace, the princess-attendant presented the king with twenty-one right ears of deer. The king then said: "Princes, ministers and wise men here assembled! You have each brought four or six or eight right ears of deer. Behold, my attendant has brought twenty-one! Therefore it is he who will become my son-in-law."

So, by the intervention of the lama, the princess acquired male sex and her union with the daughter of the king was celebrated. And the king, having become old, gave his kingdom to his son-in-law, an incarnation of Drolma!

The princess often thought: "Aka! Aka! Where is my prince and what is he doing? Here it is now more than ten years since I have lost him; I must find him!"

In a wild, flat country, the king-princess discovered a spring that bestowed special benefits to thirsty travellers. She placed her portrait over the spring and posted a guard nearby. The guard had instructions to catch hold of all men who identified the image.

One day, one of the thieves arrived near the spring. Exhausted, he drank deeply and seeing the picture, exclaimed: "Oh, there is the woman whom we carried away from the city in the country of the Muslims!" Immediately, the guard led him before the king-princess who, recognizing him as a bandit, had him thrown into jail.

A few days later, the second thief came to the spring and suffered the same fate as the first.

After a long time, the Muslim trader, now ruined, came to drink at the spring. "Aha, here is my servant!" he said, looking at the portrait. Immediately arrested, he was brought before the king-princess who heard his story: "A prince of the country of the East had sold me a beautiful embroidered picture. I had him intoxicated with alcohol, then put to sleep with a sleeping potion. I robbed him of his magic dagger, and I got hold of his companion, whom I made my maidservant for three years."

The trader, in his turn, was thrown in prison.

Very much later, the prince himself came to the spring, clothed in scraps and rags, unrecognizable. He saw the portrait: "Aka! Here is the princess of the country of the West, my wife!" The guard seized him and presented him to the king-princess. The prince did not recognize his wife but she recognized him. She made the prince relate in detail all his adventures, to tell the story of his expedition to the land of the West in search of the princess, of his misadventure at the hands of the trader, and of his life as a wandering beggar and embroiderer.

The king-princess took the prince into his service as a servant. After a few days, the king-princess said: "Prince, do you not recognize me?"

"No, who are you?" the prince-beggar replied.

"I am the princess, your wife, born in the country of the West."

The prince then, had to hear the long narration of the sufferings of the princess, of her ten years of unhappiness. So they went to find the lama-recluse, who gave her back her female attributes and made her a woman again.

The prince became the king and the princess bore him two sons. The prince also married the princess of the land where he found himself, the daughter of the old king and the wife of the king-princess, and she bore him one son. His power was immense, expanding over all the three countries together.

We have somewhat lost our sense of time listening to Karma recalling Drolma and we have not yet covered half the *nékhor*.

The Shepherd
Who Wished to Understand
the Language of Animals

If there is no harmful intent, harsh words are tolerable,
It is no disgrace to lift up one's clothing when the ford is deep.

The descent to the south is fast; we cross a little plain of flowers
and the path is well marked by its surface of white stones.
Nearby stands a large rock (*bushugsa*), before which women
who desire a child stop and make a wish. They pick up a small
white stone, putting it near their breast as if it were a newborn,
they rock it, give it food and even spank it!

Pemba says: "Some years ago, two women of Barbung made
the *nékhor* of Shey. Both of them wanted to have a son. They
each took a stone and carried it along. After some time, one of
them thought that this was not useful and she threw her stone
away. But the second woman secretly picked it up. On their
return, the second woman gave birth to two sons and the other
never had a baby."

At the base of a circle of rocks is a small lake called *La-tso*,
"Lake of the Life-force," and on the heights above are some rocks

resembling familiar religious objects, such as a lama's drum, a conch, a hand-bell. It is here that Lama Trutob Sengé Yeshé, in meditation, built a *chörten* of rock crystal. From here one can see the cave where the hermit-lama meditated. At the point where the path turns toward the southeast, a *chörten* marks the site where young pilgrims dance. The path then descends a steep slope and leads to a temple dedicated to Drolma. The exterior of the temple is painted red and the interior is very dark. On entering, the statue of Drolma is on the left, almost covered with ceremonial scarves and necklaces of turquoise and coral, gifts put there by pilgrims.

Nettles grow vigorously around this place. A lama-hermit was nourished by them and now they are called "nettles of the Pious Uncle." It is customary for pilgrims to collect them to make a soup that gives strength and is a blessing.

Near the temple there are two shelters for meditation, surrounded by junipers and dwarf rhododendrons.

The path continues over a small pass, Rigsum Gompo La, the pass of the Three Protectors.[18] On the pass is a *chörten* and visible here are impressions in stone left by the knees of Lama Trutob Sengé Yeshé. From the pass, it is possible to see the confluence and the group of temples of Shey. It is said that the pious pilgrim who makes this pilgrimage thirteen times can, on the thirteenth time, see from here the summit of the sacred Kang Tisé.

We return very late to Shey. Lama Trutob Sengé Yeshé, the originator of the *nékhor*, was, in truth, not mistaken in his choice of this itinerary.

———————

We leave Shey early in the morning. Karma, tired from yesterday's efforts and not much used to carrying a pack, asks a *drogpa* based at Shey to assist him with it for the day's march.

The trail to Samling initially passes through a landscape rent with cliffs on which dwarf birches are growing like a crust. Norbu murmurs: "If the road is long, set out with a horse; if you wish to live for a long time, take a wife of noble birth; if the summer day is long, eat a lot."

In contrast with the first part of the journey, now the slopes are gentle with scattered growths of stellaria, their stems ending in tufts of numerous blue and pink florets, their presence proclaiming the grazing grounds of Nang-khong. The son of Lama Tulku of Nijung, out searching for four wandering horses, comes to meet us.

A herd of wild goats browse near the trail, these animals almost as fearless as domestic ones.

"Why are they not frightened by our approach?" I ask.

"No one hunts them! We are in a place protected by the deities of the *nékhor* of Shey mountain. It is a refuge for all of the wild animals, who know this well." At this time, birds are numerous here; elsewhere in Dolpo, they are more rare.

"Since we are discussing animals," Karma says, "here is what happened to the crow..."

A crow and a frog were friends. The crow lived at the top of a large juniper; the frog lived at the foot of the tree. The crow flew here and there, all day long, in search of food. The frog thought, "Ah, but the crow is intelligent and crafty. If only I could be like him!" The crow had other ideas: "Why don't I just imitate the peaceful life of my friend, the frog?"

One day, the crow asked: "Friend frog, how do you eat?"

"I eat the air, the wind that blows, by opening my mouth," said the frog.

The crow decided to do the same, and passed the entire day with his beak open. Evening came; he was very hungry and said irritably: "Frog, I have followed your advice. I have swallowed the wind, but I am not satisfied. Besides, I am so weakened that I am not able to fly any more. Therefore, I am going to be forced to eat you."

The next morning, just as the crow was about to eat the frog, the frog spoke: "Crow, don't kill me at the foot of this tree; it is the place where my father was born!"

The crow took the frog in his claws and put him on a rock.

"Crow, don't kill me on this rock. It is the place where my mother was born!"

The crow then took the frog to the middle of a large plain.

"Ah, don't kill me here," the frog pleaded. "This is the place of the congregation of the frogs, and a curse will fall upon you!"

The crow then carried the frog to the edge of a little stream and the frog said: "Before you eat me, you must make an invocation to the Four Cardinal Points."

The frog took advantage of this delay to jump into the water and thereby saved himself.

Our next halt is for a meal and this time Karma speaks of the pastoral life:

Long, long ago, in Tibet, there lived a family who possessed much wealth. They bore the name of Gyuchugpo, "Great Richness." Their flock of sheep was looked after by a single shepherd, very pious. Before taking any food, he would always offer a little to his protective saint, Urgyen Rinpoché.[19]

One day, a man dressed in white appeared to him: "Why have you not offered me a part of your food today?" he asked.

"I did not dare because I had only scraps left by my master's guests," was the shepherd's reply.

"I see that you are pious and good; offer me something every day, even if it is only scraps. It is the intention that counts. Now I would like to do something for you. What would you like?"

The shepherd, who loved nature and all the things of the earth, reflected, then said: "I would like to understand the language of animals."

"So be it," said Urgyen Rinpoché, for indeed it was he. "I give you this power."

When evening came, the shepherd returned home and put the flock in the enclosure. However, his master decided to celebrate the Tenth Day by slaughtering a fat ewe. The next day, the shepherd led his animals to the pasture and as he could now understand the language of the animals, this is what he heard:

"Bee." (This was the word of the mother.)

"Mee." (This was the word of the lamb.)

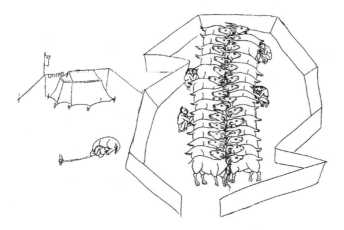

"Tomorrow, don't walk at the front of the herd; don't be greedy and don't go up too high or the wolf will eat you," the mother warned. "And don't stay in the rear, the shepherd will throw stones at you with his sling."

"Ama, where will you go tomorrow?" asked the lamb.

"Tomorrow, the master will kill me and offer my flesh to his guests," said the mother. "This is the reason for which I give you this advice: don't walk ahead of the flock, nor at the rear."

The shepherd understood these words, and asked himself what to do. In the evening he returned, very sad. To save the life of the ewe, he fled, taking with him the mother and her lamb.

Along the road, he met a horseman followed by a colt.[20] The horseman was speeding his mount.

"Mother, wait for me!" said the colt.

"Little foal, go slowly, a needle wounds me in my side. It is concealed in the saddle carpet."

The shepherd understood these words and stopped the horseman.

"Stop and dismount from the saddle, you are wounding your horse," he said.

"You stop me at the time my father is about to die! I am on my way to look for a doctor and a lama."

"Inspect the seam of your saddle carpet before you continue on your way," the shepherd insisted.

The horseman looked and found there a needle that he had forgotten to take out and he thought to himself, "This man is a lama or a magician!"

"Please come with me, you will know how to cure my father. Come!" he begged.

"I am not a lama, I haven't any power," the shepherd replied.

"You understand the language of the animals, so come!" again begged the horseman.

The shepherd was thus compelled to follow the horseman. In the house, the shepherd said to himself, "How am I to convince this man that I am neither a lama nor a doctor?"

Now in this house there were a cat and three kittens. The horseman had offered a plate of meat to the shepherd, and the mother cat said to her kittens: "Wait a little, I am going to ask this lama for some of this meat."

"This lama, what has he come to do here?" asked a kitten.

"Our master is ill. The lama has come to take care of him," the mother answered.

"What is our master suffering from?" asked the kitten.

"Our master suffers from this: he has some ants in his ear."

And the shepherd understood all these words!

"And to cure him, what must be done?" asked the second kitten, who was curious.

"It is necessary to gather the most beautiful flowers of the mountain; put them near the ear, sprinkle them with some water and some milk; then strike the little cymbals, and in this way, the ants will think, 'It's spring, the fragrance of the flowers is fresh and strong; it rains, the thunder growls,' and the ants will come out of the ear."

The shepherd understood all this and in gratitude gave the whole plate of meat to the mother cat. Then he went to gather the most beautiful flowers and followed the cat's words. He asked the master of the house for a vessel filled with some water, some milk, and for the little cymbals. Then he placed the flowers by the sick man's ear, he sprinkled them with some water and some milk, he struck the cymbals, and he murmured, "Mamoma, mamamar," for he didn't know any prayer and he spoke as he would speak to his sheep.

The ants thought, "Well, it rains, the flowers are blooming; it's springtime!" One of them came out of the ear and called to the others.

The master of the house recovered immediately. "To say that I have spent so much money in ceremonies, appealing to the lamas and the pious for a cure that was so simple!" he said to himself and he gave his house, his field and his flock to the shepherd who understood the language of the animals.

Somaki and the Three Keys

In the summer, the clouds are to the south;
In the winter, the clouds are to the north.
Black and round clouds announce rain;
Thin and long clouds announce snow.

Early in the afternoon, we pass by the houses of Tra, and then follow an irrigation canal that leads to a large rectangular reservoir. This part of Dolpo does not have much water, and the little there is must be carefully collected and stored. Below the collection tank are fields of barley and mustard. We are close to Samling. Now, the prayer walls no longer carry the sacred mantra *Om mani padme hum*, but instead *Om matri muye sale du*.

Samling is an important center of the Bön faith.[21] This religion, which distinguishes itself from Buddhism by virtue of its ancient Tibetan roots and by its unique liturgy, is, in fact, a branch of the latter which has assimilated the canonical works and iconography of Buddhism. As for the sacred representations, it should be noted that all traditional images are inverted right to left (or vice versa), that is, if the Buddhist representation of a deity has the deity holding a lotus in her left hand, in the Bön representations she will hold it in the right hand. The branches of the swastika that adorns the great *chörten* at the entrance of Samling are oriented counterclockwise. Bön devotees turn the prayer wheel counterclockwise, likewise they circumambulate sacred shrines counterclockwise.

The "Mountain of Copper" dominates the little valley, and on the valley floor is a group of temples of modest and somewhat ramshackle appearance.

The lama who is head of the community receives us and offers us hospitality. We know him because he comes to Tarap twice a year to meet with his colleagues there and to exchange wool and butter for barley.

We are put up in the kitchen of the principal temple. The lama, while drinking the tea prepared by Norbu, tells us how his ancestor, Lama Yantön Chenpo, who came from the distant region of Kham in eastern Tibet, had subdued the demon of the "Mountain of Copper," transforming him into a guardian *tsen*.

When approaching Samling from the south, we had observed the chaos of the high rocks which make up the slopes of the western side; this confusion of rocks is believed to be the result of the fight between the lama and the demon. It is said that this *tsen* is the guardian of a large area which is forbidden to hunters. Now, the wild goats thrive here in safety.

An officiating monk offers the evening butter lamp and chants his prayers to the sound of the drum. "He repels demons who roam about outside the *gompa*," says Norbu.

I ask Karma if he knows a story of demons. He pauses a little, reflecting, then relates:

> On the heights above a valley similar to that of Samling lived a demon named Atsing. He had a very old wife from whom he decided to free himself; for he had seen a girl, young and beautiful, who was living with her mother in Do, the lower part of the valley, at the confluence of two streams.
>
> The demon went to ask for the girl's hand in marriage, but the mother said, "You will not have my daughter unless you can tell me her name."

The demon, who did not know the girl's name, asked himself what he should do. On the road, he met a wolf.

"Uncle Wolf, there is something I want to propose to you. If you find the name of the girl who lives at Do, I will give you plenty of flesh and blood."

The wolf went down to Do and, at night, listened at the door of the house. "Somaki, it is time to sleep," said the mother to her daughter.

Immediately the wolf left, repeating, so that he did not forget: "Somaki, Somaki, Somaki...."

Arriving at the river, he was unable to cross over at the ford. So he leapt over, but the jump made him forget the name of the girl!

"Well, Uncle Wolf, have you heard the name of the girl?"

"Yes, I have heard it, but in jumping over the river, I have forgotten it," replied the wolf.

"Stupid! Go quickly, listen again. I will give you much flesh and blood," said the demon.

The wolf heard again: "Somaki, sleep!" and returned to the demon.

"Quick, Uncle Wolf, what is her name?"

But so abruptly did the demon put the question to him, that the wolf again forgot the name. The wolf then said, "Tomorrow, when I come back, don't put any questions to me, don't disturb me in any way, and I will tell you the name."

The next day, the wolf was able to repeat the name of the girl, and the demon went to meet the mother. The mother had to let the demon take Somaki, but she entrusted her with three grains of barley and told her: "When you find yourself in difficulty, offer these three grains of barley; the first to the Kunchog; the second to the deities of the water (*lu*) and land (*sadag*); and the third, you will eat."

The demon set up Somaki in his house at the upper part of the valley and entrusted her with a copper key. He left to hunt, and Somaki, intrigued, opened the room with the copper door with the copper key. There she found a large quantity of *tsampa* and corn flour, enough to feed an entire village.

The next day, again leaving Somaki, the demon went off to hunt and entrusted her with a silver key which opened the silver door. In this room Somaki found heaps of treasures; silver ornaments and jewels of great value. The third day, the demon left to go hunting and entrusted a gold key to Somaki, which opened a golden door. Here Somaki found only skeletons of men and animals, and corpses in various stages of decomposition. In one corner, there was an old woman, the wife of the demon, who was not yet dead.

"Girl, what are you doing here?" asked the old woman.

"The demon kidnapped me and took me for his wife," replied Somaki.

Then the old woman spoke again: "The same thing happened to me a long time ago. I am old now, and the demon locked me in here to get rid of me. If you want to save yourself, take this turquoise image of Drolma, which has special powers, and put it on the head of an old dead woman who is here. The bones and flesh will disappear and you will be dressed in the skin of the old woman."

Somaki followed this advice, put the image of Drolma on the head of the corpse and the bones and flesh disappeared, leaving only an empty skin. Thus dressed, she fled and took refuge far away, toward the foot of the valley.

On his return, the demon found the house empty!

Meanwhile, Somaki arrived in the land of a wise king who had lost his wife. She was hired as a maidservant to carry water.

Now the king was looking for a wife and had asked his wise minister to help. Somaki, in the skin of the old woman, was suffering an outbreak of lice and fleas. So, one day, believing she was alone, she removed the skin and bathed herself. But a maidservant witnessed her beauty, bedecked in jewels of gold and turquoise, and told the minister what she had seen.

The minister sent for Somaki and ordered her to destroy the skin which covered her. To all present she appeared beautiful and adorned with jewels. The minister thought: "Such a girl could only be from a good lineage; she could even become queen of this country." The king then married her.

Not long after the wedding, Somaki gave birth to a son. The son was extraordinary: he had a head of gold, back of silver, legs of copper.

The minister immediately sent a message to the king: "A son is born to you; he has a head of gold, a back of silver, legs of copper. You alone can give him a name!"

Now the demon had heard talk about this extraordinary infant and thought: "This is certainly the son that I have had from Somaki." So he stationed himself on the road along which the messenger would pass, and substituted a false message for the true one: "King, your son is born; he has the head of a scorpion, the back of a toad, the body of a snake. What is to be done?"

The king, receiving this false message, was struck with consternation and gave this order, "Kill the son and drive Somaki to the end of the world."

The minister, not able to understand the king's reply, advised Somaki to flee with her son. Somaki returned to the lower part of the valley where she was joined by the demon who, in a rage, cut the son in two, throwing one half toward the lower part of the valley, the other half toward the upper.

Somaki went back to the house of the demon. Again, one day she took the golden key, opened the door of gold and asked for advice from the old wife, who was still alive. She replied to Somaki:

"If you wish to destroy this house, lay the image of Drolma on all the skeletons in this room."

Immediately revived, the skeletons set the house on fire and on his return the demon found nothing but ashes.

Somaki fled, and again she was overtaken by the demon. Then she remembered the three grains of barley: the first grain she offered to the Kunchog, the second she offered to the *lu* and *sadag* divinities and the third she swallowed. No sooner was this done than a winged horse named Tapo Tseldang Kyangpo came down from the sky, picked her up and put her down on a desert-like plain. The demon tried to follow them but was stopped by a hot, scorching wind.

The winged horse then said to Somaki: "You must kill me, you must remove my skin which you must stretch out on the ground, legs pointing to the four directions, cut my body into pieces, place my head on the skin, also my lungs and heart and scatter my entrails all around. Then you will have good luck."

Somaki, however, refused to kill the horse. Nevertheless, it died a little later. So she cut it up, stretched the skin, put the head on the skin, the legs laid out pointing toward the four directions, the entrails scattered all around and the lungs and heart placed on the skin. Then she went to sleep.

From the earth a marvelous *chörten* came up: the lungs and heart transformed themselves into gold and turquoise; the entrails into coral; the hairs of the mane and of the tail into fruit trees. Seated before the door of the *chörten*, a ferocious dog prevented any entrance.

Meanwhile the king had questioned the minister and discovered the treachery of the false message. The king was then unable to reconcile himself to Somaki's disappearance and set off in search of her, wandering like a beggar.

He arrived on the great plain where previously nothing grew, saw a marvelous *chörten* and thought, "This must be the palace of Somaki, incarnation of Drolma." The king stopped near the *chörten* and the ferocious dog, the incarnation of the winged horse, permitted him to enter. Somaki was astonished to see that the ferocious dog permitted the visitor to fondle him!

"This ferocious dog has never let a person pass. How has he permitted the beggar to come in? He must be a holy man," said Somaki.

The king recognized Somaki, but she did not immediately recognize him. However, his gold ring proved that he was her husband, and so they were finally reunited.

The Tail That Talks

A smoking fire can still give warmth;
A bone with a little meat is delicious.

Leaving Samling, we walk for three hours before we reach Pijor. The slopes of the valley are bare; gramineous and umbelliferous plants grow only along the irrigation channels. The green fields of wheat and those of buckwheat (which takes on a rose tint) contrast with the grey-brown of the bare earth and the deep blue of the sky.

Pema Tondrup, whom I had met this past winter in Tarap, gives us hospitality. He is a *magpa*, a "son-in-law," in one of the wealthy houses of the village. "A very difficult position," he confides. His wife has not had a child and he will not be accepted as a full member of the family until he is a father.

We go to offer butter lamps at the monastery of Lang, situated about an hour from the village in a gorge at the base of a cliff. It consists of several buildings and the principal temple, founded by Tzugna Rinchen, possesses two sets of manuscripts, the *Dō* and the *Yüm*.[22]

The custodian of the temple, an old man, informs us:

> A very long time ago, the sacred volumes of *Dō* and
> *Yüm* had been removed by the traditional leader of Dolpo,
> who at that time lived in the valley of Barbung. A man of
> little faith, he sold these manuscripts to a Thakali of
> Tukucha. As soon as this unpropitious action took place, the in-
> habitants of the Barbung fell seriously ill. The books were
> then brought back to Dolpo, and were being transported
> through the valley of Panzang, when a violent wind arose.
> It was the time of the harvest and the wind carried away
> the grain with the husk, destroying everything. The books
> were then taken to Shey, where the monks then fell ill;
> then to Tra, where the wind burst forth again. Finally the
> books were packed onto yaks, which of their own accord
> took the road to Pijor, stopping only at the very door of
> the temple of Lang!

Next door, another building houses a very large prayer wheel,
a meter in diameter and more than two meters high. To gain
merit, one must lie flat on one's back underneath the cylinder
and make it turn by pulling on leather handles attached underneath the cylinder. Each turn causes a little bell to tinkle.

We return to Pijor and spend the afternoon on the roof. As
the sun is strong, we take shelter under the awning roof. Karma
needs to repair his boots. He cuts two threads the length of
both his arms extended. Then, fixing one end and twisting the
other end, he causes them to twirl together into a single heavier
thread. Earlier, he had put a piece of yak hide to soak in order
to make it soft. He then cuts off a piece and using an awl, makes
holes in it along the edges. Finally he stitches it on to the sole of
the boot. Meanwhile, Norbu has bought a leg of dried mutton.
Seeing the amount of meat on the bone, Karma laughs and exclaims: "The goat's tail was larger than this leg!" He then proceeds to tell us the story of the tail that talks:

Once upon a time, in the highlands, there lived an old man and an old woman whose only possession was a single goat. One day they quarrelled with each other, and decided to separate. But the question arose: "What to do with the goat?"

"It has to be divided into two," said the old man, hoping to get the largest part. "Woman, you hold the goat by the head, I will take her by the tail, and we will then pull, and it will break into two!"

The wife pulled by the horns, the man by the tail. The old man heard a cracking sound and thought: "Oh! The tail is detaching itself! I won't get anything at all!"

"Old woman," he said quickly, "I have changed my mind. I prefer the ribs. Come, grab the tail, I will take the head."

The two of them tugged again, and finally the old woman pulled off the tail. The old man went off with all the rest.

The old woman now had nothing for herself but the little tail of the goat. What was she to do? She put it on the beam above the hearth, saying, "The eve before the New Year, I will put the tail in a soup of nine ingredients, *guthug*, the soup that brings good luck, and I will enjoy myself."[23]

The eve of the New Year came, and the woman took down the tail to cut it up into little pieces.

"Don't cut me into bits," said the tail. "What is gained by putting me in the soup? I am so small, and without a bit of fat!"

The old woman, astonished to hear a goat's tail talk, said: "If I do not put you in the soup, I will drink only clear water!"

"Do not cut me into bits, I can be very useful to you!" the tail continued. "I can get for you all the food that you wish for."

Now, all she possessed was a little *tsampa*, begged from her neighbors, and a young calf.

The little tail then said: "Old woman, let me go. I will bring *tsampa* for you."

The old woman allowed herself to be convinced and the tail went off.

On the way, seeing a trader who was guiding a mule, the tail hid itself under a stone. The trader had stopped to make a fire and prepare tea, and the tail led away the mule loaded with *tsampa*. The tail returned with the loaded mule to the old woman, and knocked at the door.

"Old woman, open up. I return with a load of *tsampa*!"

The old woman said: "*Kunchog sum!* The goat's tail has returned! As you are so small, you can come in through the crack under the door!"

"Old woman, the load is very bulky, so open quickly!" said the tail.

The old woman, incredulous, thought: "This tail exaggerates. I am going to punish it," and she took up some cinders and a stick in her right hand, before opening the door. There, before the door, she saw a large sack of *tsampa*.

"What are you going to do with the cinders and the stick?" asked the tail suspiciously.

The old woman lied: "I was going to give the calf a blow with the stick to make her move from the door so that you could enter, and to scatter the ashes on its urine so that you did not slip...."

The old woman was now able to satisfy her hunger, which she had not been able to do for many, many months. Later, one day, she had a desire for meat, and she said to the tail:

"You must get me a little meat."

The tail left, and on the road, she met five thieves. Quickly she hid herself under a well-dried cake of yak dung.

The thieves were amusing themselves by throwing stones and one of them said, "Let's aim at that dried up dung cake."

The tail heard these words. "Don't throw stones, there is someone under the dung cake," she called out.

"What is this voice?" they said, and lifting the dung, they saw only the little tail of a goat.

"Who are you? What are you doing here?" they demanded.

"I am a goat's tail, and I am looking for some meat to steal," the tail replied.

"Good, let us then be off together," said the thieves.

They arrived near a wealthy house. Night came and the servants brought the yaks into the enclosure and, counting them, put the *dri* in the courtyard near the house.

"Keep your distance, while I go into the enclosure," said the goat's tail, who moved up and selected a beautiful yak with a red coat, then another, very fat, without horns.

"Which do you want, the red yak, or the yak without horns?" the tail asked.

The robbers cried: "*U-yu, u-yu.*"[24]

The master of the house, hearing "*U-yu, u-yu!*" stirred, thought of thieves and sent his servant out to investigate. The servant didn't see anyone, just the hornless yak who was wagging its tail from side to side because the goat's tail had affixed herself on its tail. The tail was then able to loosen the ropes that tied up the hornless yak and lead him away.

The thieves killed the yak and cut it into pieces. The tail asked for the bladder and said, "I am going to the pass, to be on watch to see if the servants of the rich owner come."

Having reached the pass, the goat's tail blew into the bladder, then let the air escape from it. This made a terrifying noise, and she called out in a loud voice: "I haven't stolen anything, but there are robbers on the plain."

The thieves, hearing these words, ran away, abandoning the body of the yak. The tail carried the meat to the house of the old woman. Thus, the goat's tail supplied the old woman with food, and she became strong and comfortable, to the great astonishment of everyone.

Eventually the king heard about this. Wondering about the old woman's sudden wealth, he sent for her. Trembling, she related the whole story. The king did not believe her and told her: "If, in three days, the goat's tail succeeds in stealing from me my priceless turquoise, my *la-yü*, I will give you land and wealth."

The old woman went back home.

"What did the king say?" the goat's tail asked, and the old woman reported the king's challenge.

"Well, we will see who is going to succeed," said the goat's tail.

The king, suspicious, had made arrangements to protect the turquoise. He had dogs tied at the four corners of the palace, he placed guards armed with sticks all around the throne, he ordered the indoor servants to keep the hearth fire going, and decided that during the night he would take turns with the queen holding the turquoise in hand while the other slept.

A day and a night passed without incident. The second night, the goat's tail went to the palace. She entered by a little hole in the wall, detached the dogs and led them into the sheep-fold, and then tied up sheep in place of the dogs in front of the palace doors. The guards were asleep and the goat's tail tied their long hair together. Then, coming to the hearth, she removed the cinders and put human excrement in their place. A lama was in the palace, reading a sacred book. The tail tied a heavy stone to the end of his shawl. Finally, she came close to the king and waited.

The queen was holding the turquoise. As she was about to fall asleep, she said to the king: "I am about to go to sleep. Here, you take the turquoise."

The goat's tail, which had come close the queen, imitated the king's voice and said: "Give it to me."

And, as soon as the tail had the turquoise, she called out: "The turquoise of the king; it is I who have it!"

Everyone woke up and the king demanded: "Where is the turquoise?"

"I gave it to you," the queen told him.

They searched everywhere, but in vain. The servant scattered the cinders to renew the fire, but immediately withdrew her hand in disgust! The guards, held together by their hair, could not separate themselves. The lama, with an abrupt movement of the hand, flung his shawl around his shoulder, and the stone tied to the shawl hit him full on the forehead, knocking him unconscious. The king gave the order to release the dogs, but the guards only released the sheep.

The goat's tail arrived at the house of the old woman with the king's turquoise, and the king, convinced of the power of the old woman, gave her, as he had promised, land and wealth.

The Myna Bird

*When three men work together in unison, they are able to accomplish
amazing things; they will even be able to convince you that your goat
is a dog!*

Our hostess, Pema Tondrup's mother-in-law, is a real gossip!
Soon, life in Pijor has no secrets from us. However, it is also
true that Karma has a way of making people talk! He always
appears to be giving his full attention, shaking his head and
uttering little surprised sounds. Handiwork also encourages
conversation and the sharing of confidences. To give the appearance of being busy, our hostess picks up a basket of fleece
and separates the white from the brown, talking all the while.
The latest story concerns a young *drogpa* who has kidnapped a
girl from Pijor. The village assembly and the parents of the girl
are demanding the payment of compensation, or the return of
the girl.

"*Drogpa*'s crime, men's wickedness!" says the hostess.

And Karma, a smile at the corners of his lips, speaks up:
"Have you ever seen the myna bird that can talk like a man?"

A myna bird was in her nest at the top of a sandalwood
tree. Agu Nedzo, a male parrot, who came from far away,
one night took refuge from a storm in this tree. At daybreak, the myna said: "What are you doing in my home?"

The parrot replied: "I lost my way in the course of the storm last night, and found shelter in this tree."

"I don't like males; go away from here," said the myna.

"Why don't you like males?" he asked.

"Males are wicked, they despise females!" she replied.

"Females are as bad as males!" he returned.

"Listen, Uncle Parrot. Listen to a story of a wicked male," the myna said.

Long, long ago, in the high land, there was, in a rich family, a very handsome son. One day, the boy set out and went down in the valley where the people of humble origins lived. Here lived a girl who was fifteen years old and beautiful, and the boy fell in love with her.

"What is your father's name, your mother's name, what is your clan, your birthplace, your work?" he asked.

"My father and my mother are metal workers; their work is looked down upon," she replied.

"I want you to be my wife; I am rich and of noble birth," he said.

The girl said, "I am of low birth; you want me now because I am beautiful, but later, you will throw me away."

"I will never do this, I am my own master!"

The boy almost lost his mind because he wanted the girl so much. He called the men of the valley together and said: "I wish to marry this girl. If she refuses, I will die on this spot."

The men of the valley begged the girl's parents to give their daughter to the young man.

At first, the boy stayed three months at the girl's place. Then he thought of returning to his home with his young wife, who had put on her most beautiful ornaments.

Reaching a forest, they went to sleep; but the boy woke up and thought: "I am going to arrive at my home with a girl of low birth. My parents and friends will abuse me, I will not be permitted to enter my own house! I will kill this girl now, take the jewels, and throw her body into the water."

With his sword, then, he struck his wife's neck, took the jewels and, thinking she was dead, threw her body into the river and went off toward his home.

The wife, who was only wounded, lay for a whole day in the water, and was rescued by a hunter who passed by.

"What happened to you?" the hunter asked.

"Last night, a thief struck me, stole all my jewels, killed my husband, and threw me into the water."

"Go back to your country," the hunter advised her.

Returning to her home, she told her parents: "A thief attacked us in the night, killed my husband and stole my jewels."

The parents anxiously asked, "What has become of our son-in-law?" and the girl stayed with them.

The boy returned to the highlands. His parents were overjoyed, for the jewels he brought increased their wealth, but he soon lost all his wealth drinking and gambling with his friends.

Two years passed. His fortune squandered, the boy thought: "I will go to my wife's parents. I'll tell them that she is in good health, and that a daughter has been born, so they will be happy and will give me some money."

He left then and arrived at the house of his parents-in-law, where he found his wife. "What shall I do?" he asked himself.

His wife said to him: "By what good luck were you saved?" The parents, happy that their son-in-law was safe and sound, proposed: "Both of you stay with us."

Two months went by; the boy again wished to return to his parents, taking his wife with him. Along the way, he again stole her wealth and abandoned her. A man of the valley from which the girl had come found her wandering, and she told him what had come to pass.

"My husband is wicked; I should never have married him."

"You are of humble birth and you should have married a man of your status," he remarked. "Stay with us now."

And that is what she did.

"Uncle Parrot," said the myna bird finishing this story, "as you see, men are born wicked, and only do evil deeds. Go far away, quickly; leave my nest."

But Agu Nedzo, the male parrot, in his turn told the following tale:

In olden times, in India, at a place called Kanpur, there lived a powerful king. This king had a son who had two friends, the son of a minister and the son of a trader.

One day, the son of the trader, who was married, received a message from his in-laws, requesting him to visit them.

The three friends set out for the trader's village. On their arrival, the king's son and the minister's son stayed in the inn of a very hospitable woman who sold good barley beer.

At that time, they noticed an old woman seated nearby who was looking at them and weeping.

"Old lady, why do you weep?" they asked.

"Seeing you, I can tell that you are two sons of noble birth. You have taken hospitality in the home of a demoness. She has a snake in her belly and when a man enters her home, he does not come away alive. That is the reason for my tears! She makes a guest drink beer, and in the night, the snake comes out through her nose and kills the man. Then the demoness steals everything that is on the dead body."

The king's son, attracted by the demoness, went in; but the minister's son stayed outside. In the middle of the night, the king's son saw three snakes come out of the nostrils and mouth of the demoness, which he killed, one after the other. The serpents were the protectors of the demoness' life-force and in the morning, the king's son found the woman dead. "What shall I do?" he exclaimed. But already, some men came and grabbed hold of him.

"What is going on here? Why is this woman dead?" they demanded.

"I slept with this seductive woman, and I found her dead this morning."

He was put in prison.

The minister's son thought: "This is an evil country." One night he saw the trader's wife go out toward the forest. He followed her to a cave where there lived a demon, pretending to be a religious hermit.

"O king of magicians! My husband has come. I have given him some food and made up his bed," said the trader's wife.

"Why did you not come sooner? You are an evil-minded woman," and with a snap of his teeth, the demon bit off her nose.

The woman fled, and the son of the minister killed the false hermit.

"I no longer have a nose," she cried. "What will become of me?" During the night, in bed with her husband, she cried out loudly, "He is killing me! He is killing me!"

Her attendants came and asked many questions. She accused her husband. "He has cut off my nose with his teeth," and the trader's son was thrown into jail.

The minister's son continued to travel through the country.

He came to a temple and he took a little rest behind the image of the deity. Three thieves entered the sanctuary. One of them prostrated himself and said to the image: "You are a powerful deity, help us to steal the king's gold and silver. If we succeed, we will offer you the king's daughter as a sacrifice, but if you do not help us, we will set this temple on fire."

The thieves went off. Aided by the malevolent spirits, they got hold of all the treasure of the king, and led the captive daughter to the temple. At the moment they were about to sacrifice her, the minister's son killed all three.

"You are a good man, and courageous," she said. "Help me return to my home."

He accompanied her up to the door of the palace.

"Come, I am going to tell my father that you saved me."

"I can't remain," he said, "I have much to do."

"Even if you are very busy, stay just a little with me," she replied.

"I have only helped you like a brother would," he told her. The girl, who desired the minister's son, cried and rent her clothing. Some servants came and seized the boy, taking him for the thief of the treasure.

Thus the three friends found themselves in the same prison.

"Tomorrow, the son of the king will be executed," said one of the guards.

The son of the king requested that he be heard by the king: "I am accused of having killed a woman, but it was a demoness. I have only killed three snakes which came from her nostrils and her mouth. These snakes served as protectors of her life-force. The bodies of these snakes are hidden under the stone of the threshold."

After the king verified this fact, the king's son was released.

The king then resolved to have the nose of the trader's son cut off. The minister's son told the king what he had seen, and the body of the false hermit was discovered in his cave. He even had the nose of the girl in his mouth! Thus the trader's son was released.

The minister's son was then questioned about the theft of the treasure.

"Three thieves got hold of the daughter of the king and the treasure. I saved the girl but she was filled with desire and wanted me to become her lover. I refused and she then hid the truth."

Behind the image in the temple, the king's treasure was found.

Then the king was convinced of the mischievousness of women, and threw his daughter into prison.

"This is the story told by the parrot Agu Nedzo," says Karma. Norbu then asks Pema Tondrup's mother-in-law if she has understood. Then follows a series of gay and sharp remarks.

Karma, a smile on his lips, goes on:

In Tarap, a father had an unmarried daughter. The daughter became pregnant. "What am I going to say to my father?" she thought to herself. She then said: "Father, I am pregnant because, being thirsty, I drank the water of a spring and I swallowed a fish with golden eyes."

To this the father ironically replied: "I would like to see the spring from which this water came!"

Is this a true story or has Karma made it up just for the occasion? It leaves our hostess without anything more to say!

The Lama and
the Queen of the Witches

If a person is the offspring of a demon, the whites of the eyes are red.

We are accommodated in the upper story of Pema Tondrup's house. In the morning, we are awakened by a cat and by the sounds of tea being churned. Members of the family pass by with their blankets as they go to spread them on the roof terrace to drive out the fleas, and some carry back a few pieces of wood for the hearth.

Pema Tondrup's wife sets up her loom in the enclosure in front of the house. Every night it is dismantled and rolled up, for one must never leave a loom "unprotected"; demons could take advantage of the night to continue the weaving in their own style. The warp, twelve arm-lengths long, is spread out and one end is anchored by some heavy stones; the other end is attached to the weaver by means of a leather strap which is passed around the body. The weaver, seated on a sheepskin, stretches the whole apparatus by leaning backwards. Pema Tondrup's wife weaves a woolen fabric, of which the weft is a coarse thread. This gives a thick cloth. "The cloth of the poor," says Norbu. We visit the *gompa* of Sakya-Gon, situated to the north of the group of houses of Pijor. The *gompa* contains the texts of the "Kanjur" and of the "Tanjur."[25] The custodian of the temple tells us this story:

> In the valley of Karmarong, situated to the west, an epidemic of smallpox was raging, and the king of the land of the West, Sonam De, called the lama of Pijor in order to fight this calamity. The Lama organized a big *kurim* ritual, and the evil stopped of its own accord, outright.
>
> Thankful, the king told the lama to express a wish. Without hesitating, the lama asked for tax exemption for the four valleys of Dolpo for eighteen years.
>
> The wish was granted and with the money that would have been paid as tax, religious works, printed in Lhasa, were bought.

Karma adds:

> I have heard it said that near Tashilhunpo there is an image of Champa, similar to that in the *gompa* of Sakya-Gon. Lama Shang was the custodian and had taken vows of celibacy. The time came to consecrate the image by putting precious objects inside. However, it was noticed that the interior of the statue was occupied by a large number of demons. Lama Shang thought a long time, then he asked all the villagers to join together, clothed in their most beautiful apparel, to blow trumpets and flutes, and to shake in all directions the tails of white and black yaks. "Lama Shang is going to get married! Lama Shang is going to get married!" they shouted.

The demons, hearing the commotion and the shouting, all came out of the image to see what was happening and they rejoiced when they heard that their enemy, the lama, was breaking his vows.

Thus Lama Shang made use of their departure from the statue to deposit the ritual offerings within it and to seal the opening.

Returning to Pema Tondrup's house, Karma tells us of the misfortune that women can cause to men, especially those women who are witches. "Not far from Lhasa, there was a valley where all the women were witches," Karma says. According to Karma, when a man is occupied with eating, should one of the witches arrive, he falls ill. Witches are said to bring about their victim's death by stealing from them the *la*, the vital spirit. Karma continues:

There was, then, in this valley, a very rich family. The mother was a witch and would absent herself in the middle of the night, after having been, as all witches are, normal during the day. This woman was the queen of the witches.

One night, the son saw his mother seat herself on a wooden trunk and fly away. Intrigued, the next day he hid himself in the trunk before his mother departed. "This trunk is indeed heavy and does not go fast!" his mother said to herself. But they arrived, in spite of this, on a great plain, near a tree where all the witches of the region had gathered.

The mother seated herself on a throne of moss and received gifts of skulls, hearts and human blood. One witch also offered a brain, but the queen had forgotten her spoon. So she stretched her right arm, which became longer and longer and longer, so that finally it was able to enter into her home, where she picked a spoon off the shelf. Then the arm returned to its normal length and the queen of the witches could eat the human brain. Later, she returned to her house astride the trunk, as though on a horse, her son still hidden inside it.

The next day, the mother was busy spinning woolen thread and her spindle fell through the opening in the roof terrace down into the kitchen. "Son, go fetch my spindle!" The child, who had seen the woman's arm lengthen, said: "You need only lengthen your arm and you can pick up the spindle. You have the power to do this!" The mother, furious, realized that her son had guessed that she was a witch. She covered him with her apron and gave him a powerful blow on the head, which changed him into a dog.

So, the son turned into a dog but he kept his human mind and his understanding of the language of people! He wandered for a long time. One day, he heard villagers praising the saintliness of a religious man named Lama Shang.

He came to meet Lama Shang as he was about to make the circumambulation of a *chörten*. The holy one immediately perceived the true nature of the dog, and said: "Dog, I know that you are a man but I don't have the power to return you to your true form. Go, then, to Lama Ralotsawa; he alone can do this." Then he attached a gold coin between the dog's two eyes.

Lama Ralotsawa, while in deep prayer, had a premonition of the arrival of a creature in difficulty. He instructed his servant: "A creature, undoubtedly human, is in difficulty; receive him and inform me."

The servant, who expected to see a man arrive, saw only a dog come and he chased it away. The dog hid himself behind the hermitage. In the evening, the Lama inquired about his visitor.

"No man came, only a dog came and it has hidden itself behind the building."

"Go look for this dog. It is he whom I must free from possession, from him I must remove malevolent forces."

Lama Ralotsawa was holding a *torma* in his hand and when the dog appeared, he threw it in the direction of the dog's head. This caused the gold coin, which had been attached between the eyes, to fall, and the dog resumed its human form.

The child, freed, then related his miseries.

"And your mother, where does she live?" asked the lama.

"My mother lives in the country which is called Pempo. She is a witch, in fact she is the queen of the witches, and her trunk serves her as her steed. She changed me into a dog after covering me with an apron and striking me on the head. It is Lama Shang who understood that I was a man. He told me to go and find you, and fixed the gold coin on my forehead. I am grateful to you for having restored my state as a man."

Lama Ralotsawa kept the boy as his attendant. After two years, he thought about the boy's evildoing witch-mother, and said to himself that it was necessary to suppress her.

"Go and see your mother," said the Lama.

"I will not see my mother; she is a witch with great power," the boy replied.

"Take this yellow scarf and go see your mother. If she gives you something to bring, do not open the package!"

The boy returned home and said to his mother:

"I am your son. I was turned into a dog, and I have again become a human being, thanks to Lama Ralotsawa, who gave me human form."

The mother said: "This lama must be very powerful; I wish to offer him a present," and she entrusted her son with a triangular iron box which contained a thunderbolt. "And, whatever you do, do not open it along the way."

The boy thought: "The lama told me to not open anything. On the other hand, my mother must intend that the contents of the box will harm the Lama. I must protect my master by releasing the contents of the box now. The scarf will protect me." He opened the box and the thunderbolt fell out, but the scarf protected him. The boy became afraid, and thought: "My mother is indeed a wicked witch! She wants to kill the lama."

When he returned, his teacher asked him:

"What did your mother say?"

"My mother gave me an iron box and told me not to open it along the way and to offer it to you. I understood that she wanted to kill you with the contents; so I opened it and a thunderbolt fell out, but the scarf protected me."

Three months later, the boy returned to his mother; the Lama, aware that the death of the witch was approaching, said to the boy: "If your mother gives you a gift, whatever you do, do not open the package!"

The mother, seeing the boy arrive, thought to herself: "The box, opened in the Lama's presence, had no effect. I am going to send something even more powerful." And she showed great joy at the coming of her son.

"Take this very big package to give to the holy man, but whatever you do, do not open it in the course of your journey."

This time, the boy did not open the box and handed it over to the Lama. The lama asked him to return to his mother, place the gift close to her, and open it, and then to leave as quickly as possible: "Your scarf will protect you!"

The boy returned to his mother. That night, as soon as she went to sleep, he put the box close by her, opened it, and fled as fast as he could go. Huge clouds billowed out of the box and nine times a bolt of lightning fell on the house. The mother died, crushed under the ruins.

"Since that day," says Karma, "there are not many witches in the land of Pempo."

"How can one know that a woman is a witch?" asks Norbu.

"A witch has warts on her face," says Karma with conviction.

"In Dolpo, there are no witches," says our hostess. "There are only a few mischievous spirits of dead people."

Karma goes out of the courtyard, cuts a particularly thorny branch of wild rose, places it on the doorstep and builds a *towo* on it. This will repel evil spirits—demons and witches. We fall asleep after Karma's prayer.

The Nine Tricks
of the Hare

To say that there is no truth to a proverb
Is to say that there are no wrinkles on the arse.

In the morning we leave Pijor for Po, the next inhabited place
on our itinerary, to visit the sacred retreat of Shang Rinpoché,
one of the most important shrines in Dolpo, which Kagar
Rinpoché had particularly recommended we visit. The long
climb above Pijor takes us through abandoned fields, abandoned no doubt due to lack of water. In flower here are numerous thorny plants which make yellow patches on the bare soil.

Very few villagers of Pijor ever go to Po, our host had informed us; for them it is "the end of the inhabited world." Actually, in Po there are only six houses and little cultivation, and
the people pay no more than three silver coins in taxes each
year, an indication of the relative significance of the place.

The distance between Pijor and the hermitage of Po cannot
be covered in a single day. At the end of the morning, after
having crossed two passes, we see Po to the north, but a major
obstacle is before us: the gorge of the Panzang Chu, which flows
more than thirteen hundred meters below us.

The weather is beautiful and the horizon is fringed by the line of lightly snow-covered ridges that separate Dolpo from Tibet. After our descent, we cross the river by a cantilever bridge. We have no choice but to camp at Lhalung, at the river's edge. This is clearly a traditional halting place, judging by the stone hearths and the numerous flat stones on which loads are placed to protect them from the damp earth. Norbu is uncomfortable with this campsite. Souls of the unlucky, who perished while travelling, wander in the world of the living, haunting the junctions of trails, precipices and the environs of bridges. For protection, *towo* are built around the campsite. Norbu lights a big fire and, from time to time, throws on a branch of juniper. The pleasing incense is likely to attract the favors of the local deities and to repel malevolent spirits.

Taking advantage of this halt, and to put a stop to Norbu's anxious comments on our choice of campsite, I ask Karma: "How did humans become intelligent?" as I had been thinking for some time that his views on this subject would be interesting to hear.

"It is the hare that is crafty, sly, facetious and wise," he says.

Long, long ago, in nomad country, there lived an old man and an old woman. Their home was a small tent. All they possessed was a small clay cooking pot, a sheep and a goat. The old man grazed his two animals every day on the heights, and the old woman stayed alone under the tent.

One day, the old woman gave birth to a child. She wrapped it in rags, anointed its fontanel with oil, then went to find some wood.

A hare, sly and mischievous, entered the tent, killed the baby, removed the head, and ate the body. Hearing the old woman returning, he put the head on the bedsack and put a little *tsampa* on its nose and lips. The old woman saw the hare escape and noticing the traces of *tsampa* on the infant's face, she thought, "Father hare, you are kind, you have given my baby something to eat," but when she lifted the child, she saw there was nothing left but the head. The old woman, in tears, went to inform her husband: "The hare has killed our infant! It was a reddish-brown hare."

The old man left to look for the hare. Seeing a yellow one, he said: "You, yellow hare! How have you managed to be so yellow?"

"I ate yellow grass and drank yellow water." And the yellow hare was able to save himself.

Farther on, the old man saw a reddish hare.

"Reddish hare, how have you become reddish?"

"I became reddish eating red grass and drinking red water." And the reddish hare escaped.

At last, the husband saw a reddish-brown hare.

"Reddish-brown hare, in what way have you made yourself reddish-brown?"

"It is from eating the infant of an old man and an old woman that I became reddish-brown."

The old man seized the hare and put him in his garment, to carry him to his tent. On the way, tired, he sat down and went to sleep. The hare took the opportunity to flee, and put, in his place, a large piece of ice.

The old man woke up, took the load to the tent and upon arriving called out: "Wife, be quick, prepare the fire and heat the cooking pot full of water; I have brought the reddish-brown hare."

The old man took the piece of ice out of his garment and threw it into the cooking pot. Finding his garment damp, he thought, "The hare has urinated."

The two old people then waited for the hare to be cooked, but found instead that it had disappeared!

Again the husband left on a search. He met a yellow hare and a red hare, and he asked the same questions as before. At last, he found the reddish-brown hare and seized it. He decided to kill the hare there and then.

"Old man, don't kill me here, I will go with you to your tent," said the hare.

The old woman put the pot on the fire and the old man prepared to kill the animal when it said to him:

"Old man, in order to kill me, you each must take a bar from the loom: you, old man, with a *urlu*; you, old woman, with a *tashing*. Then sit down facing each other. I will then jump between you two and you both can strike me."

The old people agreed, but they didn't strike quickly enough and the hare was able to jump aside while each of the two old ones gave the other a mortal blow.

Karma goes on:

A hare and a tiger became friends. The hare was intelligent, but his conscience was base and he could only think of killing the tiger to get his skin.

One day, the hare invited the tiger to join him. He lit a small fire by the edge of a cliff and gave the tiger a place to sit between the fire and the cliff edge. Then, slowly, the hare began to feed the fire and the fire grew and began to radiate more and more heat. The tiger drew back more and more. Finally the tiger fell backwards over the cliff, roaring and howling as he fell.

"Tiger, my friend, don't cry, you have all my sympathy," called the hare.

The hare set out again and met a tea merchant to whom he said: "My friend the tiger is dead at the foot of the cliff; I will sell you his skin."

The trader, laying down his load, went to skin the tiger.

The hare, seeing a shepherd, called out to him.

"Shepherd, would you not like to go and find a load of tea, abandoned on the edge of the road?"

And the shepherd, leaving his flock, went off to find the tea.

The hare then went to find a wolf.

"Friendly wolf," he said. "What would you say to a feast of ewes?" And the wolf devoured the flock of the shepherd.

The hare then said to himself: "I must get rid of the wolf," and went to find the ram, Tugpo Tashi and the billy-goat, Rapo Tarkyé. He asked them:

"Tell me, are you two strong enough to kill the wolf that has consumed the herd?"

"How can we kill a wolf?" they asked. "We are not strong enough."

"You, Billy-goat, you stand erect on your rear feet and knock the wolf with your horns, and you, Ram, you take a huge stone and strike the wolf."

The wolf came, the billy-goat stood erect, but the wolf jumped at his breast and removed the goat's heart! Then the ram charged the wolf, but the wolf led the ram to fall into a deep hole which broke its back. So the wolf saved himself.

The hare was disappointed at the failure of his plan for killing the wolf.

Arriving at a stream, he filled a saddle bag with sand. The wolf asked him: "What are you doing?"

"Tomorrow, the king will give some sheep to one of my wolf friends. This bag will serve as my saddle, as I am to ride this friend to take myself to the king."

"I would like to be this friend," said the wolf.

The hare then saddled the wolf, and thus mounted, went to see the king.

A servant saw the hare arrive, riding on a wolf. He called some men armed with bows and arrows. The hare fled, but the wolf, weighed down by the bag, was killed.

Karma goes on with the tale of the cunning hare:

In a pasture, the hare saw a wild yak, then a hunter. The hare told the hunter about the yak: "I am going to stand by the yak in order to point it out to you," he said.

"Uncle Yak, a man is coming, don't fool about. Quick, we must leave," said the hare. The hunter fired at the yak and the yak fell on his back and made several somersaults as it died.

With the last kick, the hooves of the yak caused a stone to fly up, which shattered the nose of the hare and killed it. The hunter carried away the flesh of the wild yak, and left the body of the hare to the carrion-eating birds.

After a silence, Karma adds: "The hare can also be an incarnation of the Buddha."

A man had only a small field of barley. He was hoping to get married with the money he received from the harvest. But a hare came regularly to eat the barley. One day, the man set a trap and caught the hare.

"You are destroying my only wealth. Moreover, this field of barley must serve to pay for my wedding dowry!" said the man.

"Don't kill me," the hare begged. "I will help you to get married. If you have confidence in me, then go to the summit of the mountain and consult the wise hermit hare who is there. He will give you good advice."

The young man went up to see the hermit hare, who was, in fact, the same one who was devastating his field.

"Holy hare, what must I do to find a wife who is wise and of good birth?" the young man asked.

"Leave the barley to the poor hare that you took in your trap and I will help."

At the time of the harvest, there was nothing left in the field except for three little sheaves of barley from which the young man made *tsampa*. He then loaded up his donkey and set off with the hare, who had become his friend. They went to find the young man a wife.

They arrived in the capital of a prosperous land. The hare poured out a little *tsampa* in a nearby lake and the donkey drank there.

"Here is a man wealthy enough to feed his donkey *tsampa* in great quantity!" said the king's servant who had watched the scene, and he went to report this fact to his master.

Then the hare secretly removed all the silk banners from the palace, tore them up and spread them on the ground, shouting: "The prince of a faraway country has come to ask for the hand of the king's daughter!"

And the king gave his daughter to the man so rich that he fed his donkey *tsampa* and walked upon silk.

Then it was necessary for the young man to return to his own land. The king, his subjects and the young couple went off in a procession making a great clamor.

The hare, who preceded them, went to find a demoness who lived in a house filled with gold and turquoise, and said to her: "Demoness, the king of a powerful country comes to make war on you. Hear the shouts and this terrible commotion. Hide yourself, quick!"

"Where can I hide myself, friend hare?"

"Here! In this copper cooking pot," he replied.

The demoness hid herself in the pot and the hare closed the lid and lit a big fire. Then he roasted her.

Thus, the hare was able to offer a palace filled with gold and turquoise to the young man who possessed only a small field of barley.

Karma laughs: "I am thinking of the hare. As a sly deceiver, he is like Chang Apa. His eye is similar to that of a cat, his ears are similar to those of a mule, his mouth is similar to that of a dog, his teeth are similar to those of mice, his paws are similar to those of sheep, his tail is similar to that of a goat and his shoulders are similar to those of a man. His progeny are as numerous as those of the wild goose and when someone beats him, he shouts like a man!"

And after another silence, Karma, as a practical man, adds: "The skin of the hare is worthless; it cannot be tanned because it is so thin, like paper."

Karma reflects a moment, then with a voice full of malice he says: "The cleverest one of all is Chang Apa! His intelligence is as great as the hare's and he plays tricks on people in order to make them more intelligent! He lived a long time in the country of the Middle."

Chang Apa had borrowed a very large sum from a *drogpa*, while on the pilgrimage route to Kang Tisé. He promised to return it to him quickly. One day, as he was circumambulating the large prayer flag pole at Darchen, Chang Apa saw the *drogpa* coming toward him. Quickly, Chang Apa took hold of the pole.

"What are you doing there, Chang Apa? Don't you know that you must return the money I lent you?"

"I am very busy now. I have a most important task, I am holding up the sacred pole. If you want your money back, you must hold up the pole in my place, so I can go and get the money."

The *drogpa* agreed and Chang Apa instructed him: "Hold the pole with both your arms and keep your eyes fixed on the top. If you see it move, shout: "The central pillar of the religion is going to fall!"[26] so people will come to help you.

The *drogpa* watched the top of the pole. He believed that he saw it move, though it was only clouds floating by. So he shouted at the top of his voice: "The central pillar of the religion is going to fall!"

The pilgrims that were present, thinking it was a joke in bad taste by a sacrilegious fellow, mercilessly beat up the poor man, and made a fool of him while Chang Apa was already far off.

On his way, Chang Apa met some children fishing in a stream. The children had rambled off some distance. He took the fish they had caught, fried them and ate them. Then he put each of the skeletons into the holes of field mice.

Coming back, the children looked for the fish. Chang Apa told them they had escaped, and had gone into the holes of field-mice.

"If you don't want to believe me, look over here, only don't come too close. Here, let me do this," and delicately, he drew out the skeletons from the holes.

"Somebody has eaten the fish!" said the children.

"It must have been the field-mice!" said Chang Apa.

The soles of Chang Apa's shoes were full of holes, and he needed a little hide to repair them. On the road, he saw an old woman who was tanning a hide. "Here's my chance!" he said to himself, and, approaching her, he said:

"How beautiful you are! and not a wrinkle on your face!"

The old woman passed her hands over her cheeks, and Chang Apa, taking advantage of this, took the hide and fled.

Continuing on his way, Chang Apa arrived at the edge of a river and saw a horseman coming his way.

"Where are you going?" the rider asked.

"I am going to cross the river, can you help me?"

"I have to continue on my way, which is on this side of the river; but I can lend you my horse to cross the ford. He will come back by himself."

Chang Apa mounted the horse, made it enter the water and, coming to the middle of the river, stopped the horse by pulling on the reins. However, from a distance, it appeared that he was unable to make the horse cross over. Then he rode back to the bank.

"This horse doesn't want to cross. Lend me your clothes, then he will obey me, for he will then think that it is his master who is crossing the river."

Chang Apa, dressed in the horseman's clothes, then crossed over. From the other side, the horseman, naked and numb with cold, shouted: "Send back my horse and my clothes, quickly!"

Chang Apa then put some butter on the forehead of the horse and called to the horseman, "Aho! Aho!"

The horseman looked at the horse and said to himself: "That's not my horse, mine doesn't have a white spot on the forehead. Moreover, the rider doesn't look like the man to whom I loaned my horse." And he waved to Chang Apa to go on.

Chang Apa had no money. He left for Lhasa. On the way, he saw a group of porters who were waiting to be hired, and sat down with them.

A wealthy trader came up and said: "I have a load of porcelain bowls to carry to my place; I will give three wise counsels as wages to the one who will transport it."

The porters all refused, excepting Chang Apa. "One can make money on any number of occasions," he thought, "but it is more difficult to obtain good advice."

"I will carry this load," said Chang Apa.

The trader and Chang Apa made an agreement and Chang Apa carried the load.

After a while, Chang Apa demanded: "Can you give me a word of advice?"

"'Don't believe the one who tells you that it is better to be hungry than to eat too much'," said the trader.

"That is good advice!"

After a while, Chang Apa asked for a second word of advice and the trader said:

"'Don't believe the one who tells you that it is better to go on foot than to go by horse'."

"That is indeed good advice," said Chang Apa.

They continued to go along and arrived in front of the trader's gate.

"What is the third piece of good advice?" asked Chang Apa.

"'Don't believe the one who tells you that there are porters more stupid than you'!" said the trader.

Immediately, Chang Apa let slip the rope of his load, which fell to the ground, breaking the bowls into a thousand pieces.

"'Don't believe the one who tells you that any of these bowls are not broken'!" said Chang Apa.

Chang Apa, walking in the streets of Lhasa, saw a beautiful daughter of a noble family. He did not hide his desire. The girl was willing, provided Chang Apa agreed to a bet, the terms of which were that he was obliged to make love to her one hundred times consecutively, one after another, in a single night, failing which he would lose the bet.

They passed the night together. Chang Apa, in order to give himself strength after each session, ate the brain of a sparrow. The girl, after the ninety-ninth time, became aware of this ploy and hid the last brain. Chang Apa, exhausted, was then not able to fully satisfy his companion-in-love the hundredth time.

As they now disagreed on the result of the bet, they decided to speak to a judge, but they could not speak openly about the true nature of the bet. So Chang Apa used a subterfuge:

"We have seen a tree covered with one hundred fruits," he said, "but this girl pretends that there are only ninety-nine. We have made a bet about it. Which of us is right?"

"There were only ninety-nine fruits!" said the girl.

Then Chang Apa said: "This tree had indeed ninety-nine fruits well ripened. But there was one that was not quite ripe." To this, the girl had to agree.

The judge reflected and then said: "A green fruit is still a fruit; this cannot be contested," thereby giving the verdict to Chang Apa!

Balabewa
the Innocent

Of a hundred horses, only one wins, even if by a head;
Of a hundred men, one by his knowledge outwits the others.

There is a silence, then a smile appears on Karma's face; no doubt he is thinking of another tale of Chang-Apa. Then, again on the theme of how humans became intelligent, he says, "Here is the tale of Balabewa the innocent, who became intelligent, thanks to some lessons he learned."

Pa Khyungpo Abchen Tsorala, a wise and powerful king, had a guileless son who was called Balabewa. The king decided to initiate his son into the affairs of the world, and sent him off to hunt.

Accordingly, Balabewa set out in search of game, travelling the endless plain on horseback. One day he saw a fox and set himself to following it, but the fox went down into his den. Balabewa dismounted from his horse, undressed himself, and tied his clothes to the saddle. Then he entered the tunnel of the den, placing his hat behind him, over the opening. The fox was able to escape past

Balabewa and came out of the tunnel with the hat on his head! This gave the horse such a fright that the poor animal fled, along with Balabewa's clothes.

Balabewa returned to his father, on foot and naked. The king insisted on hearing the story of his adventure.

"On the endless great plain I pursued a fox, entering his den after him. But the fox escaped, upsetting the horse! I will never again go hunting. It is too dangerous!"

After a while, the father asked his son to go and do some trading. He gave him a hundred fat rams fitted with a hundred empty pack bags.

Balabewa went far off, repeating endlessly: "If I sell the fat rams, what do I do with the bags? If I sell the bags, what do I do with the rams? I am not cut out to be a trader."

Along the way, he stopped to rest near a spring. A girl came, carrying a water container on her back; then a second girl came. Balabewa offered to help the younger one lift her load. While doing this, the turquoise which he was wearing at his neck fell into the container without his noticing it.

When Balabewa realized that he had lost the turquoise, he returned home, telling his father: "I am not capable of carrying out business."

His father replied: "Tomorrow, go again and keep in mind this bit of advice: 'Nourishment is less important than profit'."

The next day, Balabewa again arrived at the spring. Meanwhile, the girl had found the turquoise and had placed it on a large rock over the spring. Many girls saw the reflection of the turquoise in the water and tried in vain to catch it, thinking that it was in the water. Balabewa discovered the jewel at the same time as the girl he had helped came to the spring again.

"Where are you going?" asked the girl.

"I am going to do business, but I don't know how to begin!"

"What do you have to sell?" she asked.

"My father has given me a hundred fat rams and a hundred empty pack bags. Then he said to me: 'Nourishment is less important than profit,' but I don't know what it means!"

"But this is very simple! To feed yourself, each day you have only to castrate a ram and eat the testicles. To fill up a pack-bag with grain, you have only to shear the wool from the back of an animal and exchange it for grain!"

"You are a very intelligent girl, help me with my business," said the young man.

So the two set out together to find a rich trader and exchange wool for grain. When the hundred bags had been filled with grain, the son returned to his father's palace.

"What did you do to succeed in this trading?" the father asked.

"I met a girl to whom I confessed my ignorance, and she helped me," he told his father.

"Do you know this girl?"

"Yes, every day she goes to draw water at the spring!"

"I think she is very wise," the father replied. "You ought to take her for your wife."

The king and his son returned to the spring and placed a turquoise on the large rock over the water. Many girls tried to fish out the turquoise when they were only seeing its reflection! It was the intelligent girl who realized the true location of the stone.

The king wanted to kidnap the girl, but he was caught by the girl's parents. The king was locked up, but Balabewa was set free.

The king wrote a message to his son from the prison. It said: "I am all right. I am kept prisoner. When I ask for food, they give me a bowl of beer in the morning and another in the evening. Do what you can to free me." But this message was not legible because it was written with milk.

In vain, Balabewa showed the paper to lamas, to wise men, to the minister. Everyone thought him a simpleton as they could see no message.

Three years, three months and three days passed. One night as he was going to sleep, he examined once again the paper sent by his father. The light from the lamp shone through the paper and the letters appeared at last. Balabewa was able to read his father's appeal for help. He quickly left to free his father and met again the girl who had advised him so well in the trading business.

"Where are you going?" she asked him.

"I am going to rescue my father, who is between life and death," Balabewa said.

"I know where your father is kept. Prepare a bowl of curd in which you hide a turquoise and the jawbone of a sheep. I will take it to him," said the girl.

The girl succeeded in making her way to the prisoner. She gave him the bowl of curd, saying: "Old man, don't eat like a glutton! Drink slowly, take little sips, and hide the turquoise in the neck of your garment. With the jawbone of the sheep, cut your bonds."

The king understood this message. He found the turquoise and the jawbone. The turquoise he gave to the guard, who let him escape. He made his escape and left with the girl, whom Balabewa then married.

But Balabewa was ignorant as to how to make love. His father again gave him advice:

"Make use of the extremity of flesh which possesses articulation and which is without a bone."

That night, Balabewa counted the eighteen articulations of his body, and while making the count, he touched his penis which stiffened itself. He told himself that it was a bone. Finally he thought of the tongue. Convinced he had discovered the proper device, he thought he had made love by using his tongue.

"Last night, I made love," he told his father the next day. The father, incredulous, asked him: "How did you do it?" "I found the extremity of flesh which possesses articulation and is without a bone, the tongue, and I made love!" The father was horrified at the stupidity of his son. "Go and ask another woman so that she can teach you how to make love." But all the women in the kingdom refused.

One day, Balabewa and his wife went to a festival. Balabewa rode a stallion, his wife, a mare. While they were watching archery, the stallion mounted the mare.

"What are they doing?" Balabewa asked.

"They are making love," responded his wife. Balabewa understood; from then on he could not do anything but make love.

The father, seeing this, fastened the brain of a sheep on the door of the room, saying, "Some men die of making love too much; certain vaginas become rotten from too much love-making." Balabewa, smelling the odor of the brain, became fearful and told his wife his father's advice, and she suggested that it would be good to make love once every seven days or even every three days.

Balabewa, who had learned trade and love, became intelligent, thanks to his wife, Pumo Dongtso.

"*Kunchog sum!*" Norbu exclaims, commenting on the stupidity of Balabewa, while generously stoking the fire.

Leaving Lhalung, so-called perhaps because of the profusion of fragrant bushes that are not found elsewhere in such numbers, the trail climbs toward the little group of houses of Po. The vegetation is now scanty; some ephedra grows here and there. The fields of Po are overgrown with weeds, convolvuli and thistles, in striking contrast with those of the other villages of Dolpo, where the fields are always carefully maintained.

An old man, Tsering Chömpé, shows us the trail leading to the hermitage of Po. It takes us two more hours of walking, climbing over fallen rocks, to reach Sepug, "the cave of rosebushes," Shang Rinpoché's place of retreat.

The retreat is a small cave-dwelling, set in a huge rock, and faces south. The cave is enclosed by a red-painted wall. It is also a temple and contains images of Champa, "Buddha of the Future," and Padmasambhava, of which the largest is life-sized. These are placed on a set of shelves carved in the rock that forms a wall of the temple. On each side of the images are stacks of manuscripts, each carefully wrapped and kept between two wooden boards. At the foot of the images, a pilgrim has made a donation of all his ornaments. There are some red ribbons and ornamental tufts (ornaments usually fixed on the long braid of the *drogpa*'s hair), an ivory ring, a piece of shellwork of round shape, a little silver reliquary, a copper seal ring, and a silver-ornamented fibula. To the right of the images is the lama's seat, and a conch and a bronze *dorjé* are placed on a little bench nearby. Karma and Norbu clean the interior of the temple and replace the holy water in the vessels.

This mass of rock dominates all Dolpo, and it is from this place that the powerful Lama Trutob Sengé Yeshé "took off" to open the pilgrimage of Shey. To the north, rows of mauve-violet ridges rise up; beyond them, snow-covered peaks, the mountains of the Changtang.

On the little terrace in front of the temple, all the wildflowers appear to have congregated. Wild roses, white mulleins, dwarf willows with pale green foliage, and blue thistles all abound.

Sitting in front of the hermitage, Karma tells us a story which he had heard from a Sherpa of eastern Nepal. The Sherpa was on his way to Mount Kailash to sell some *dzo* which he had brought from the land of Khumbu.

In the high valley of Khumbu lived a holy man called Buddha Tsenchen, who was nearly a hundred years old. Now it is believed that the life of a holy man will not go beyond a hundred years if he is not married, and the villagers wanted to look after this holy man for the longest time possible. So, some villagers came to persuade Buddha Tsenchen to marry a maiden fifteen years of age. The girl bore marks identifying her as a *khandro*.[27]

Tsenchen lived then a good many more years to the benefit of all. He had exceptional powers and spoke freely to his tutelary deities, to Urgyen Rinpoché and to his *polha*, and the deities responded to him.

In the vicinity resided the local deity Tritsen Karpo, one of the attendants of Urgyen Rinpoché.

One day, the old lama appealed to Tritsen Karpo: "There is no salt in the land of Khumbu, and the salt that comes from Tibet each year is very costly; could you procure a store for us?"

"The time for this has not yet come, but I promise to help you."

"Whether the time comes or not, I will make a prayer," said Buddha Tsenchen.

"If you wish, we will speak of it seriously each day, but this must be done far from all other people."

The lama then bought a little field and asked his wife to cultivate it. This was done in order to keep her occupied and away from the house so he could meet the deity alone.

The next day, the wife prepared the meal, left the cooking pot on the hearth, covered the embers with ashes to prevent their smoking, and left to work in the field.

That day, Buddha Tsenchen and Tritsen Karpo talked at length about the salt. Then the lama made a ritual burning of juniper to honor the deity. From the field, the wife saw white smoke rising in the sky and said to herself: "Look at that, the fire is still smoking, though I left the embers well covered!"

The second day, Buddha Tsenchen and Tritsen Karpo continued their conversation, and again the smoke of the juniper rose above the house. The wife became concerned, and then suspicious.

The third day, she took particular care to cover the embers with ashes before leaving for the field. Again the deity came and again the smoke from the burning juniper rose in the sky. The wife then ran toward the house and saw, leaving by the window in a hurry, an apparition clothed in white, with a white headdress.

"Who has come here while I was in the field?" she asked.

"Woman, you are too suspicious! I will not tell you, neither tomorrow, nor the day after, but I will tell you after three days."

"Then it was a woman who came to see you?"

"I will tell you everything after three days," was all the lama would say.

The wife, furious, took the porcelain bowl from which the deity had drunk and threw it at the lama's head.

"Woman, since you want to know what has happened here, this is it. For three days, I have been in conversation with Yul-lha Tritsen Karpo on the subject of a store of salt for our country. Now, this cannot be realized because of your jealousy and your folly, and the whole country is going to suffer because of it. And now I am going to die in three days. If you want to bring blessings to the country, live a virtuous life and retire to a place of meditation."

The holy man died as he had predicted, and Khumbu never had a stock of salt.

Without too much hurry, as if with reluctance, we depart from the hermitage among the flowers, seemingly suspended from the heavens, and we head back to the bridge over the Panzang Chu. We will spend the night again by the bridge.

The End of
the Demon
of the Cave

At the edge of the water, construct a towo *of three stones.*
A bird perches itself there; snare it, pluck its feathers, eat it.

Karma gets up before dawn. He strikes the tinderbox, lights a
fire and makes tea.

Breaking our camp at Lhalung, we climb the trail. On the
way, we collect some ammonites that Karma calls *shidag gi
khorlo,* "almanac of the local divinities."

Arriving at the abandoned fields of Karang, we take the trail
to Ku, along which artemisia grows. This plant, when dried
and powdered, is effective against lice.

We reach the summer grazing grounds of the village of Ku.
Scattered about are huts with dry stone walls and flat roofs. We
visit one of the huts. A low door gives access to a single room
without any other opening. Inside the room are stone shelves,
a hearth, and the utensils needed to make butter—buckets,
wooden scoops, ladles, and a goatskin—all hanging from a
beam. Outside, children keep watch over animals grazing in
the pasture.

The houses of the village of Ku are well-situated below the main trail. The crossroad is marked by a *mendang*, a long prayer wall. Next to this we leave a part of our loads which we protect with a *towo;* this keeps away inauspicious spirits and makes thieves hesitate. In this treeless area, we are surprised to see a large walnut tree growing near a cluster of houses.

A villager, Mémé Tsaldung, is aware that we are making a *lingkhor* of Dolpo, and he shows us around the village temple where, unfortunately, the paintings, which are exquisite, have been damaged. Our host recalls the brief visit of Lama Jamgön Lotrö to Ku. The lama, originally from the distant eastern province of Kham, while passing through Dolpo had, in a dream, the revelation that he must "open" a pilgrimage to the mountain Ngodrup Ri, near Ku. But when he visited Ku, he unfortunately saw a woman busy relieving herself. As this was highly inauspicious, the lama returned without carrying out his plan.

We talk about the divinities, and especially about the unpredictable role of the *tsen*, who, according to our host, are numerous in this valley. In fact, storms here are very violent, and the divine anger is often felt (lightning is linked with the *tsen*).

Karma relates:

> In the land of Tö, a family was very wealthy; they had fields of barley, a large herd of yaks and pack-goats. Two sons were born; the older took up trading; the second attended to the herds.
>
> One day, one of the goats climbed a cliff. The shepherd followed the goat and came across a crack in the rock. He entered the cavity and discovered a series of large rooms ornamented with gold, silver and turquoise. Succulent dishes were laid out and he tasted them. This was the palace of a *tsen*. The *tsen* came in unexpectedly and the boy hid himself behind a door. The *tsen* detected the smell of human, closed the door and discovered the intruder. "I have need of a servant, and behold, one is found!"
>
> Days went by and the boy's parents grew more and more anxious. They made appeals to lamas and offered very costly ceremonies. Finally they received news through

a divination: "Your son is not dead, but his life is perpetu-
ally in danger. He is under the power of a *tsen*. The *tsen*
has given him custody of three keys, of gold, of silver and
of copper, which give access to the treasures of gold, silver and copper."

A magician (*ngagpa*) was called. He wrote the name of
the *tsen* on a piece of paper which he put into a triangular
box. This would utterly destroy the *tsen* from a distance.

The *tsen*, knowing that his doom was desired, gave the
boy a hat that made him invisible and sent him to the magician. The boy was instructed to put a little bird's feather
on the end of the magician's pen and a little dust in the
triangular box. Thus the *ngagpa*'s action was neutralized.

Many days later, a second *ngagpa*, one-eyed, was consulted. He performed a ritual. Then the *tsen* said to the
boy: "Today, a very powerful magician has arrived. You
go again, fix a little feather at the end of his pen, and throw
a little dust in the triangular box."

The boy did what he was asked to do. The one-eyed
magician noticed the dust, and because he had only one
eye, he was able to see the feather, which he removed from

the end of the pen. Then the one-eyed *ngagpa* wrote the name of the *tsen* on a paper which he put into the box, and performed a *kurim*. Then he called the *tsen* by shaking a black cloth.

"Boy, I must go to the powerful magician. I will take myself there in the form of a pigeon. When you see me, you must carefully close the sleeves of your garment to hide me."

The boy, invisible, went near the magician and saw the pigeon arrive, lured by the force of the magic. The bird entered the front of the *ngagpa*'s garment and came out by the sleeve, then went to hide himself in the boy's garment. But the boy had forgotten to close the sleeves. So, the bird had to come out again and was utterly destroyed by the power of the *ngagpa*.

By another ritual, the *ngagpa* was able to free the boy from the *tsen*'s control and in this way, the boy was able to obtain the riches of the *tsen*.

"The cave of the *tsen* reminds me," Karma adds, "of another story. This story is about the cave of Saka Drigpug, which is near here, on the main trail from Changtang to Lhasa. It is said that this cave is haunted by a particularly evil demon."

The wind was blowing with great force on the plain; an old man and an old woman had found shelter in the cave but were stripped of everything and without food.

A little later, a caravan of traders from the distant province of Kham arrived. The old ones hid themselves at the back of the cave. The men of the caravan placed the loads of the pack animals in a heap at the entrance of the cave, lit a fire, and began to prepare tea and a meal. The two old ones were terrified, cold, and half dead from hunger. But the old man was crafty. He asked his wife to undress. Then, with charcoal, he drew ears, eyes, and eyebrows on her buttocks. Then he asked her to walk on all fours and to move backward in the direction of the cave entrance. So well did she do this that the attendant who first saw her was utterly terrified. Panicked, he rushed toward his friends, shouting: "The demon of the cave of Saka Drigpug is threatening us; it has a rounded figure, black eyes like charcoal, and instead of having a human mouth, it has a vertical slit!"

And everyone fled, leaving the old people something to eat and a fire to warm themselves by.

"May there be kindness for all! *Tashi sol*," says Karma.

The Three Children
Who Were Saved from the Water

Do not make offerings on the first day of the Sixth Month;
These will then benefit the demons and evil spirits.

It is now ten days since we left Tarap. From Ku, we climb up to
the Yesi-la, where the trails to Po and Pijor, coming from the
west, meet with those from Lhori and Karang, our next halt.
The view is magnificent. At a lower level are two fields of
mustard, a dazzling yellow, and by them, a house: "That is
Mirang. A man lives there by himself," says Karma.

Late in the evening, after crossing over two ridges, we reach
the heights above the village of Karang. The wife of the village
headman receives us. Her husband, Chigyab Ngodrup, is away
at the temple where the men are preparing a ceremony.

From the roof terrace where we are installed, we enjoy a com-
manding view of the village and its temples situated at a lower
level. Numerous channels bring water to the fields from the
stream which cuts the cultivated area into two. Fields of mustard, buckwheat and barley alternate.

This evening, at my request, Karma finds the energy to tell
another story.

In ancient times, in the land of the East there was a powerful king, the father of three girls, and in the land of the West, there was also a powerful king, who was a widower. The minister of the king of the West was constantly pressing him to marry again.

In the West also lived an old woman, an able cook, who knew, above all, how to prepare tripe very well. The minister asked her for matrimonial advice, and she went to the land of the East to investigate.

The daughters of the king of the East were always seated on the roof-terrace of the palace, watching from afar the palace of the king of the West.

"If I become the wife of the king of the West, I will make uniforms for a thousand warriors from a cubit of fabric," said the eldest.

"If I become the wife of the king of the West, I will give a measure of grain to a thousand warriors from a single measure," said the second.

"If I become the wife of the king of the West," said the last one, "I will have three children born at the same time."

The old woman heard these words and reported them to the minister, who then encouraged the king to ask for a daughter of the king of the East in marriage.

"I give you the youngest," said the king of the East.

"No, I want all three," replied the king of the West.

"If you want all three, you will have much trouble!" the minister warned.

The king of the West insisted, and married the three sisters. The two elder ones did not keep the promises they had made. Only the third kept her word, and gave birth to triplets.

Now the older wives were jealous and they decided to get rid of the newborn children. Nearby a dog had given birth to three puppies. The sisters replaced the babies, two boys and a girl, with the puppies, put the babies in clay pots and threw them in the river.

The king became furious on hearing that his wife had given birth to puppies and had her put into prison.

The three pots floated on the river, going with the current as far as a confluence, where they stayed, motionless, in a whirlpool.

A saintly man, who went every day to bathe in the river and fetch fresh water, saw the three pots. He pushed the pots aside so that he could draw water, but they returned and put themselves in front of him!

"When I remove these pots, they come back in front of me!" he remarked.

The lama lifted them out and discovered the three children, whom he took home. He fed them and brought them up in the Religion.

Eventually, the queen was judged, and the minister pronounced the judgement: "To the queen, three puppies were born; their father, then, is a dog. It is necessary to kill her for this grave crime." But the king decided to keep her locked up. As for the older queens, they never kept their promises and they had no children.

Twelve years went by, and one day the lama told his wards: "I am now going to retire to meditate in a cave; each day, make a little food for me. This flower, Drolma Metog, which I entrust to you, will bloom as long as I am alive. When it withers, I will be dead. Remember my advice: always stay in this hermitage, do not go to the land of the West to play, and do not eat food that strangers offer you."

The lama also gave them three excellent horses. He added: "Later, indeed much later, from the dried-up flower, a new flower will be born, and when it opens, I will reincarnate myself in the form of a bird, Chapo Karabshog. The bird will be born very far from here, but it will always be your protector."

"Our father and mother, who are they?" the children asked.

"Now I will not say anything, but when I come back in the form of a bird, you will meet your parents," the lama replied.

The lama stayed a long time in meditation, isolated from the world.

One day, the flower suddenly withered. The children thought: "The flower has dried up, our lama protector has died. What shall we do? The lama had indeed said, 'Don't go to the land of the West.'"

The two boys, who were very handsome, went about on horseback. One day, they participated in a race, which they won, as they won every time, defeating the chieftains of the valley and the king's minister. The king, present at the race, asked them:

"Which is your country and your lineage? What is the name of your clan?"

"We have neither father nor mother, no name as progeny or of clan. Our protector, a saintly lama, is dead, and we live at the lower end of a remote valley."

The king and the minister knew of the lama, and wondered how he could have children, as he had made a vow of celibacy. "These boys are well-behaved and strong. Who are they?"

The king and the minister remained perplexed, but the older queens remembered their misdeed and guessed, "They are, without doubt, the children of our sister. They must be destroyed, they must be poisoned."

The eldest queen instructed the old servant to prepare a plate of tripe, to which she added some poison, and had it carried to the hermitage in the distant valley. The old woman arrived safely and gave the plate to the girl. "This old woman came from far away with this food. We must accept it in order to please her," she thought, but she waited for her two brothers. She then divided the tripe into three portions.

In the house, a mother cat had three kittens. One of the kittens ate the three portions and died immediately. Seeing this, the girl remembered the instructions of the lama. "This meat had poison in it. Someone wishes us harm," she decided.

Three days later, the boys returned again to the festival. Seeing them, the two queens thought, "Our poison was not strong enough. The children are still alive." The old woman was again sent with a plate of tripe. The girl did not eat any, but made three portions of it. The second kitten ate some and died immediately. The girl again thought, "Someone wishes us harm."

The boys again took part in the horse races and carried off the prizes. The two queens sent the old woman with a plate of tripe a third time. After eating some, the third kitten died. Finally, the three children understood the plan of the queens and the old woman.

Meanwhile, the king, puzzled, continued to wonder about the origin of the children. He consulted a magician who said, "No one can tell their origin, only the bird Chapo Karabshog can do this; this bird is the reincarnation of a saintly lama. He is like a jewel which gives strength."

Immediately, the king wished to acquire the bird and ordered a search. All the servants went off in different directions but it was not seen.

Around the hermitage of the lama, the flower Drolma Metog bloomed again. "The saintly lama announced," the children told themselves, "that when the flower opened again, he would be reborn in the form of a bird. This has now happened. The bird will surely show itself soon."

The older boy left to search for the bird, far, far, up to the edge of the world. He arrived in a great forest growing beside a high cliff. There, an old woman was weaving on a loom. She was the custodian of a cave in the cliff.

"Old woman, can you tell me where the bird Chapo Karabshog, king of the birds, is found?"

"My master is a demon; he is guarded by animals: tiger, snake, leopard, and bear, and you cannot go any further. So go back to where you came from. What is it you want?"

"I want to meet the bird!" said the boy.

"Many men have come this far, but none of them has left; all have been transformed into stone. If you go further, you will die."

"This bird is my teacher, I must find him," said the boy.

The old woman then gave the child a ball of thread from the weft and attached one end of the thread to the loom. The boy left, unrolling the ball. When the thread was entirely unrolled, he came to a rock which was the door of the cave and he struck it, which caused it to open. The child went in, and saw trees with many fruits and the animal guardians: the tiger, the snake, the leopard, and the bear. At the same time, he saw countless birds. One of them said, "I am not the bird Chapo Karabshog."

A bird-liar then said, "I am the bird Chapo Karabshog." The child, who did not know how to recognize the true bird-incarnation, was transformed into stone.

Three years later, the second brother, concerned by his brother's absence, decided to take up the search. He arrived at the edge of the world and found the old woman, who repeated, "Do not go to look for the bird, unless you go to die."

But the boy did not listen to this advice. Guided by a bird who pretended to be the bird Chapo Karabshog, he went on, right up to the cave. As he too had been deceived, he was transformed into stone.

Three years later, as her two brothers had not returned, the sister thought, "Neither of my two brothers has come back, the flower Drolma Metog flowers again, and the bird has not come." So she left in search of the bird.

She saw the old woman, who told her: "Many men have passed by here, but all are now dead. Don't enter into the cave!"

But the sister entered there, unrolling the spool of thread, and she saw the birds perched on a sandalwood tree. At the top of the tree, a bird said, "As for me, I am not the bird Chapo Karabshog."

A bird-liar then said: "It is I who am the bird Chapo Karabshog!"

The girl said a prayer: "My lama protector is the bird Chapo Karabshog. I ask him to turn three times around me, making a circumambulation, and to perch on my right shoulder. May he come quickly!"

The bird Chapo Karabshog came down from the top of the sandalwood tree, three times circled around the girl, and perched on her shoulder.

"Protector bird, spirit of our lama, my two brothers and a great number of men are here, transformed into stone; give them life again!"

Then the bird perched on each of the stones, and their human forms returned to them. They all said, "Girl, you are a deity similar to Drolma. You have brought us back to life; we are your servants."

Thus, these men, ministers, warriors and servants, were freed. They mounted the excellent horses adorned with turquoises and corals, and arrived at the foot of the valley where the lama and the three children had lived.

The king of the land of the West came to hear that this faraway valley now had a queen, and that she possessed the marvelous bird for which he had been searching everywhere. Envious, he sent his army against that of the reincarnate, but was defeated.

"We are going to kill the king," said the victors.

The bird then said: "Do not kill the king; he is your father!"

"And where is our mother?" they demanded.

"Your mother is in prison."

The king listened to these words, and, repenting his error, said: "These are indeed my children."

Prostrating himself before them, he begged their forgiveness.

The queen, who had spent many years locked up, was merely skin and bones. The bird perched on her shoulder and immediately she became young and beautiful again.

"Here is the mother of the three children," said the bird-protector. "It was the older queens who replaced the three newborn children with puppies, enclosed them in clay pots and threw them into the river."

Thus the three children, succeeding their father, became the rulers of the country.

The Middle Kingdom

Beer makes words flow from the mouth;
The sun drives lice from the fur-lined coat.

We leave the headman's house early in the morning and visit the three nearby temples.

The village temple of Karang contains a large image of Champa and a series of paintings representing the life of Padmasambhava. The paintings adorn the walls of the extension of the main temple.

In the village temple the villagers are busy preparing a *kurim*, following the ritual of the *leutor*. They hope for an immediate and beneficial result from these rituals, that is, the elimination of the insects that are attacking their grain crops. Karma tells me that such a ceremony is also performed amongst the *drogpa* when the animals are covered in ticks. During a pause in the ceremony the villagers question us on the purpose of our visit.

The other two temples are situated a little to the north of the village. At Palding, Lama Angdü receives us and tells us the exemplary story of the founder of that sacred place, Lama Chökyung Gyaltsen. Then Lama Angdü gives us details on the visits of Lama Lotrö Angdü and of Trutob Tenzin Gyalpo, two religious figures who have great power.

The third temple, Yab-Yum, has been the seat of a religious school and Kagar Rinpoché has stayed there. The custodian of the temple tells us about one of the earlier incarnates who lived there:

> The lama of Yab-Yum had just died. Everyone was convinced that he would come back to earth, reincarnating himself as a human being. Did he not say a little before disappearing: "I will return to Yab-Yum"? In the course of the cremation, the smoke of the funeral-pyre directed itself toward the south. A crow, different from those usually seen in Dolpo, came and perched on the roof of the temple. A wild rose grew up out of dry soil, and blossomed in the Twelfth Month, in full winter!
>
> A little later, a pious devotee, a nun, not married, became pregnant. Several days before bringing the baby into the world, she had a dream: in a copper basin used for water, there was milk; a child appeared, carrying a golden *bumpa* which lacked the little stopper adorned with peacock feathers. He gave it to the pious nun.
>
> The baby was born with a caul. The newborn lifted its right arm in the direction of the temple of Yab-Yum, then wept. The infant was unusually mature; he walked at the age of one year. With some soil, he made *torma* figurines; he wrote *mantras* without anyone teaching him to write, and recited long prayers without them having been taught to him. The pious nun tried to hide her young son's abilities, but one day a neighbor saw him write a *mantra* and

very quickly the news spread. He was recognized as the incarnation of the deceased lama. Moreover, this was confirmed a little later: During the festival of the Seventh Month, the child, who helped with rituals in the temple, noticed the empty seat at the head of the row on the right and went and sat there. It was the seat of his "spiritual ancestor." He took up the bell and *dorjé* and officiated!

The custodian's narrative is over. Karma approaches the seat, a square box-like structure adorned at each corner with a carved motif, and with hands joined, rests his head there for a moment, then places a butter lamp before the seat and lights it.

After visiting the three temples of Karang, we leave for Saldang, which we reach after a short walk of only three hours. It is our intention to visit the nearby temples of Trakyem and Nangkhung.

Nyima Tsering, the chieftain of the valley of Dolpo, lives in Saldang, and we greet him. His house is the largest in the village and is preceded by an enclosure for the yaks, with little constructions used for storing salt, and a courtyard where mastiffs are tied, some more menacing than others.

Norbu quotes a folk saying for us:

"At the door of the rich house, four dogs stand guard, one at each cardinal point."

A maidservant dressed in a tattered *chuba*, hair unkempt, comes to calm the dogs by putting a flap of her *chuba* on their muzzles. Nyima Tsering looks through a window of the first floor and invites us to come up.

We are all seated on carpets with flowery motifs in the Gyantsé style. Nyima Tsering is the most influential and powerful personage of Dolpo. His dress sets him apart; a *chuba* of quality, black cotton bordered with otter fur, a blouse of Bhutanese raw silk, black leather boots, well-shaped for riding and decorated with red and blue leather. Casually counting his rosary, he questions us and then, in reply to my question, speaks of himself.

Nyima Tsering is one of the very few who know the history of Dolpo, and he explains the origins of his people, who descended from *drogpa* who settled in the valleys. "Besides," he adds, "I myself do not feel healthy unless I am out in the pasture, under the tent, or bartering!"

> Many generations ago, there was a king in Dolpo and his palace was at Lhori. The king Ranag (Ranag was also the name of his lineage) asked to marry the daughter of the king of Lo. The king Ranag sent his minister to bring the girl, but she died on the way, at the pass of Ser. The king Ranag did not dare inform his father-in-law. Some time later the king of Lo asked for news of his daughter, and Ranag became afraid. King Ranag made a prayer and it happened that the cow in the stable became the incarnation of the deceased and brought a son into the world who became the heir of Ranag.
>
> But Dolpo had lost its power at the time and was coveted by the king of Jumlang to the West, and by the kings of Lo and Kag to the East. Happily, Dolpo is a poor land and at a high altitude. Even today, the Nepali frontierguards do not venture into Dolpo and leave us in peace.

Nyima Tsering tells us of his lineage. He belongs to the Ombo lineage, a lineage whose mythical ancestor was a horseman who descended from the heavens.

Nyima Tsering offers us hospitality and we are installed in a room of his house that directly overlooks the courtyard and serves as a storage for salt and a dormitory for the caravan drivers. The serving maid brings us a plate of coarse *tsampa* and a jug of beer. "Turbid and lacking in alcohol," Norbu remarks.

When we are alone, I ask Karma if he has heard of beings who come down from the heavens and found powerful lineages on earth.

"The rider of the divine white horse," he replies to me, "is considered, among the *drogpa*, to be a heavenly benefactor. Although the story is not complete, this is what I have heard about him:"

Once, a horseman rode over an endless grassland. He met a shepherd and asked:

"Which way will bring me to the king of the West?"

"The way to the palace of the king of the West is along the heights," he was told.

After a little, he met a goat-herd; then a yak-herd.

"Will I arrive today in the kingdom of the West?" he asked.

"If you go fast, you will not arrive; if you go leisurely, you will arrive," replied the yak-herd.

The horseman found the reply to be incomprehensible and went off at a gallop. Soon the horse stopped, exhausted; the horseman then appreciated the herder's advice! He did not arrive until the next day near the king of the West, to whom he offered his services.

"Who are you?" asked the minister. "What work can you do?"

"I am single; I know how to do everything. Give me an old person's work, a woman's work or a youngster's work."

The first day, the horseman did old people's work, combing the hair of goats and yaks, and in less than a day he did what others found difficult to do in seven days.

The second day, he did women's work: he carried water, and churned tea while singing:

> At the bottom of the churn,
> The tea of China is good to taste.
> On the rim of the churn,
> Some *dri* butter; and mixed in,
> Salt, which is an expression of thanks.

Then he milked the *dri* and they gave much more milk than normal. All the while he kept a rhythm by this song:

> Dri, give your milk,
> With the rope, I tie your feet up.

After having milked ten *dri*, he made collars for the calves and to tether them he made ropes out of five different threads: wool, fluff, yak hair, goat hair, and fine lamb's wool. Then he decorated the collars with embroidery in red thread.

The third day, the horseman did the work of a young man: he exercised the horses. "If there are many horses and a single rider, of what use is it to make the horses run? Does this make sense?" he asked himself. Then, changing occupations, he first spun yak hair with much skill and then practiced archery.

The minister said to the king: "This man is skillful and wise; let us keep him in our service!"

But the horseman refused, citing a proverb: "The king has only limited power; the *tsampa* is not finely ground."

Then the horseman went off toward the kingdom of the East. The first day, he taught sheep shearing, singing:

> If one cuts too high, one wounds the little finger,
> If one cuts too low, the sheep is wounded.

To the women, he taught the milking of the ewes:

> Tie up the animals with one rope that comes loose
> when it is drawn upward.
> If the grass that is growing is uprooted, it dies. If
> one strikes the udder, the milk will not come
> and the ewe will perish.

To the men, he taught the making of felt:

> White felt, stretched on the ground, is useful to the
> lama in his rituals;
> And to the *lhapa* who calls the divinities;
> White felt is valuable to young married people.

And he continued on his way.

After riding for a long time, he came to a tent. "Tie up the dog!" he shouted, but no one answered. Continuing on, he came to a house, but found no inhabitants there either.

Eventually, he was stopped by a stream, and not finding either a ford or a bridge, he camped on the bank and went to sleep.

The horse ambled off. Upon waking up and not seeing his mount, the horseman went off in search of it. Helped by another horseman, he followed his horse's hoofprints, discovered the ford and found his horse, tied up near a tent. To the owner of the tent, he said: "It is my horse that is tied here!"

"Who are you, and where do you come from?" asked the man of the tent.

"I come from the country of the king of the East. Not having succeeded in crossing the stream, I went to sleep, but my horse crossed the river all alone. Give me shelter tonight."

The next day, the horseman set out again and his horse began to gallop every which way. "My horse must be a divine white horse," the horseman said to himself. Crossing over the ford again, he came to a group of tents and asked for shelter; and he carefully tied up his horse.

"Where do you come from? How have you crossed the stream?" they asked him. "No one knows the location of the ford."

"I come from the north where my horse lost its way, and I have worked in the countries of the kings of the West and the East. To locate the ford I just used, I need all the men of the encampment who should come to me on their horses and follow me," he replied.

The horseman made his horse go into the water, followed by some of the *drogpa*. They went up gently against the current and the divine horse found the ford, which was named thereafter "the ford of the divine white horse."

The chieftain of the tents then asked the horseman to build a bridge.

To build the bridge for the *drogpa*, the horseman asked as payment the precious jewel that was in their possession, an antelope horn made of turquoise!

"This bridge will bring you many riches greater than the horn-jewel, because it will give access to deposits of salt," he told them.

The *drogpa* chieftain finally accepted. "How many men will be needed to help in the construction?" he asked.

The horseman proposed to make a suspension bridge, and he insisted that he would construct it entirely by himself. On each side of the river, he built a *towo*. Then, while he recited a prayer, these piles of stones transformed themselves into the foundations of a bridge. Next, he took some sinews of yak, which he stretched from one bank to the other, between the piles. He uttered first a prayer, then the magical words "Haa" and "Huu," and the sinews became iron chains.

The *drogpa* then handed over the precious jewel to the horseman.

Karma interrupts his story, drinks several mouthfuls of beer, and takes up the story once more:

The horseman started out again, stopping in the country of the Middle. This country seemed fertile, but lacked people and animals. There he had a dream. In his dream, the king of the West appeared as a possessor of yaks, the king of the East a possessor of sheep; he himself was rich and strong with a herd of many horses. He also saw a mare giving birth to numerous foals.

Waking up, he found himself on an empty plain and looked in vain for the horses.

In the evening, he lay down again, using as pillow the saddle carpet of white felt. In a dream, he saw great riches, and on waking up, these visions became reality. The plain of the Middle was covered with animals and three-storied houses!

Meanwhile, the king of the West asked himself what became of the horseman who gave so much good advice, and he sent a man to the Middle to look for him.

This messenger arrived in the land of the Middle, and asked for advice: "Is this the road to the land of the Middle?"

"You are in the country of Middle, the king is Gyalpo Takar Mikar," he was told.

The messenger returned and reported to the king of the West.

The king of the East did the same, and came to know of the prosperity of the country of the Middle.

The king of the West, puzzled, wanted to hear the details himself. Disguising himself as a tea trader, he went to the land of the Middle with twenty-one mules loaded with various products, and set up his tent near the palace.

The horseman questioned the king of the West.

"Where do you come from? What is the name of your country?"

"I come from the country of the West. I am a trader of tea," replied the king.

"Come closer to me, king of the West," said the horseman, who had recognized him.

"Who are you?" asked the disguised king.

"I am the horseman who stayed in your kingdom; I taught your subjects to card yak hair and to make rope from animal hair."

The king of the West returned home, furious to have been shown up as curious and to have been exposed as a liar.

The king of the East, also puzzled, accompanied by a servant, went to the country of the Middle and asked to see the chieftain of the land.

"Who are you?" he was asked.

"I am the king of the East; I have come to take account of the state of the country of the Middle."

The horseman and the king of the East, pleased to meet again, spent three days together. The king of the East invited the horseman to come again to his country, to teach wisdom, saying: "With a single leap, the tiger reaches his prey; a single teaching of the king is rewarding."

The king of the East unwisely pastured the yaks, the horses, the sheep and the goats all together, and the animals died in great numbers.

On the advice of the horseman, the male yaks were sent up high in the valley, and the dri and their little ones were confined to the paddock. At the southern side, the geldings were sent to the heights; the mares and the foals toward the lower part of the valley and the stallions were kept in the middle. At the eastern side, the castrated goats were sent to the heights, the females and the kids lower down and the rams stayed in the middle.

And so the kingdom of the East became prosperous.
Then the horseman decided to go to the kingdom of the
West. The king of the West received him but did not ask
him for advice. He proposed a horse race on the plain of
the Middle to which the king of the East was also invited.

The white horse of the horseman, king of the land of
the Middle, was given great care. In the morning, he was
given the first drops of milk of one hundred *dri;* at midday, the first drops of milk from one hundred ewes, in the
evening, the first drops of milk of one hundred goats. He
was also given three handfuls of *tsampa,* some butter, some
raw sugar from Purang, and reddish-brown raw sugar
from Kyirong.

The day of the race came, and the residents of the three
kingdoms gathered. The kings entered many horses, their
heads adorned with an eagle feather and the mane with
colorful strips of cloth. The horses were ridden by boys
under sixteen years of age.

The white horse went as fast as a shooting star, and won
the race, followed by a red horse and a blue horse; all three
were the horses of the king of the Middle. The fourth fast-
est was the horse of the king of the East; and the fifth that
of the king of the West.

The king of the East did not say anything, but the king
of the West was furious and asked: "Why is the white horse
so fast?"

"Because the white horse bears the name Shooting Star."

"Why did the red horse come in second?"

"The red horse is the horse of the *tsen.*"

"And the blue horse?"

"The blue horse is the horse of the *lu.*"

The king of the West did not understand, and asked
once more:

"How is it possible that these horses go so fast?"

"The four elements, earth, water, fire and air, are under
their feet," was the answer.

The king of the West did not understand at all; neither he did have the wisdom necessary for making his kingdom prosperous.

The kingdom of the Middle became the most prosperous of all.

The riches of Changtang had been discovered by these heroes called *lhechen kachen*: "For whom all work was child's play and whose every prayer was followed by immediate fulfillment."

The Mummy of
the Lama of Shang

Among one hundred lamas, one saintly lama!

Finally, to escape the fleas that are swarming in the store-room, we move to Nyima Tsering's roof-terrace to sleep. Early in the morning, we hear the sounds of the looms in the courtyard. Four women are working there, on daily wages, and they remain seated from morning to evening, practically without taking a moment to rest. Nyima Tsering, with an old felt hat thrust over his eyes, slowly crosses the courtyard, spinning his prayer wheel and counting his rosary beads. His daughter-in-law sells us some *tsampa*. Karma remarks that she uses the "small measure" (which is used to pay the wages of servants), and not the "measure for trade" (which is larger). She has lost the latter, she maintains!

Some mustard plants are drying in the sun; they will be used to prepare soup. We are pleased with the weather which today is fair. Weather is an important part of our journey and can be a real constraint, even if walking for hours in the rain is supposed to assure the accumulation of additional merit!

The climb to the monastery of Trakyem takes half a day. Contrasting with the sloping pastures between Ku and Karang, this

section of the mountain supports no vegetation, and the shale slopes appear purplish. We reach a zone of large rocks and stone slabs which are difficult to go around or to clamber over. Suddenly, at a turn in the trail, the temple of Trakyem comes into view, standing against a cliff, the forward part on a terrace facing to the south. The present structure, I was told, is a recent construction. Nyima Tsering also told us that he gave three full grown yaks to the carpenters for all the wood required in its construction.

This dramatic site, suspended between the earth and the sky, is endowed with a perennial spring. Is this a gift from the local divinities? Trakyem is certainly the site of a very ancient hermitage.

The temple, entered through an open porch, is built on a square plan. Four large, heavy pillars support the ceiling with its richly decorated covered roof opening. On the south side, a window with crossbars, covered with paper, permits a little light to enter. The altar is set against the north wall, and is surmounted by a series of shelves containing the one hundred and eight volumes of the Kanjur, a gift of Nyima Tsering. On the other walls are murals of the tranquil and the fearful deities of the Nyingma pantheon, of Machig, "the Mother"[28] and of Padmasambhava. But what is most notable in the temple is the mummy of the Lama of Shang, who died in 1959 at Bawa, in *drogpa* country. The lama's mummified body has been placed on a structure three meters above the floor, in the center of the room. The body is arranged in the posture of teaching and is dressed in his ceremonial apparel. He appears to be giving his blessing.

Trakyem comes to life at least twice a year. During the First Month, more than thirty devotees join together to read the books of the Kanjur. In the Fifth Month, Nyima Tsering presides over a series of ceremonies called "blessings for the harvests and livestock."

We are received by Sonam, the custodian. He is one of the travelling monks that one meets in Tibet and in the valleys of the Himalaya. Born at Mugu, in Western Nepal, of a poor family, he was entrusted as "servant novice" to a lama who taught him to read and to write. He memorized the Nyingma texts, accompanied his master to the sacred Kang Tisé, made the tour of the holy mountain thirteen times, then came to Dolpo where he met Shang Rinpoché, to whom he attached himself. Short, dumpy, his skull shaved, his face flattened, he resembles a wrestler. He has been residing at Trakyem for the last three years. Observing his behavior with the wife of the Lama of Sel Gompa, who frequently visits the temple, it could be said that, here at least, the vows of chastity appear to be a little relaxed!

Sitting by the fire, we are offered tea and *tsampa*. We then give the news from Tarap. In his turn, Sonam relates to us how the mummy of the Lama came to Trakyem. Shang Rinpoché, before dying, had asked that his body be returned to Trakyem.

So, on his death, a group of faithful devotees embalmed his body and transported it from Tibet to Trakyem as soon as the passes were open. Sonam, who had accompanied Shang Rinpoché on some of his travels, and Karma, who had known the Lama very well at Shungru, have been able to piece together the principal episodes of the lama's life. This pious monk, born in Shang, in central Tibet, travelled a good deal, went on pilgrimage to India and Kathmandu; then to Kang Tisé. Arriving at Dolpo, he became friends with Kagar Rinpoché and they both devoted themselves to visiting the temples of the four valleys and to organizing their repair.

Sonam particularly remembers an episode which took place at Sandul Gompa in the valley of Tichurong, south of Dolpo: The inhabitants of this valley had adopted the practice of sacrificing rams and goats to the divinities of the mountains and the soil although it was sacrilegious to kill animals, and even more so under the porch of the temple. Shang Rinpoché organized an expiatory ceremony and convinced all the inhabitants to attend. An old woman, particularly hostile to this outsider, decided to poison him. Very early in the morning, with the first rays of the sun, she went to the lama's place with poisoned cakes. Seeing her coming, he covered his head with his scarf, thus making himself invisible! The frightened woman fled and became blind.

Shang Rinpoché also travelled to Lo and to Nyi-shang, to the east of the Kali Gandaki River. He died in the Year of the Sheep, on the tenth day of the Sixth Month, an auspicious day, after a meditation of seven days. Sonam believed that Shang Rinpoché would reincarnate himself as his behavior and deeds had been highly meritorious.

Karma explains how the body of Shang Rinpoché had been preserved. "It was placed in a wooden coffin, in the position of meditation: the legs bent, the hands joined at chest height. Three loads of salt were required for mummification; the salt was

heaped all around the body up to the level of his heart. The body was kept this way six months, then it was transported to Trakyem. The recovered salt has great virtue: it protects the herds and drives away hail."

We bed down in the temple, our heads toward the altar as a sign of respect. The room is dimly lit by some butter lamps. The presence of the body of the Lama of Shang evokes for Karma ghostly spirits. In response to my questions, he says, "Corpses who walk about like living beings are called *rolang*," and he tells this story:

In upper Tibet, a lama famous for his magical powers, before dying, said to his disciples: "When I die, it will be necessary to drive a thousand iron nails into my body. If this is not done, I will not find rest."

On his death, his disciples thought: "We cannot defile the body of our master by driving iron nails into it," and they did not obey the lama's request. The mummified body was placed on an elevated seat and clothed in the lama's most beautiful ornaments. And the funeral ceremonies began.

In the middle of the night, the monks were asleep in the temple, and the lamps were almost spent. Only a young novice was awake, being troubled by fleas. He saw the body of the holy lama raise itself. Terrified, he went outside, then stood at the window of the temple to see what happened inside. The lama made a gesture of blessing, then all the monks rose up and danced. A little before dawn, everything returned to the way it had been before.

The young monk related his experiences to the villagers, who, seized with fear, consulted a lama magician: "Our deceased lama, and all the monks, have become ghosts, *rolang*. What is to be done to be rid of them?"

"Below the village, tie a small boat of yak hide to the river bank" was the response.

Night came, the lama magician made a *kurim*. Then he opened the door of the temple, went out and all the monks followed. Upon arriving at the edge of the river, he took his place in the boat and crossed the river. The *rolang* followed him, entered the water and were carried away by the current.

Karma continues:

At Lhasa, in the Jokhang temple, in front of the image of the Buddha known as Jowo Rinpoché, there is a heavy stone under which Urgyen Rinpoché interned the Nine Demon Brothers, Damsid Pun-gu. A beam of light emanating from the forehead of the Jowo prevented the demons from crying out or escaping.

The great Lama Tsongkhapa presented a crown of five golden lobes to the Jowo Rinpoché. He placed the crown on the head of the image and it blocked the beam of light. This made it possible for the demons to be liberated. The stone rose up a little and Tsongkhapa heard a whispering. He circled the stone and heard a sound like the wind coming from beneath the stone. He thought, "There are some beings trapped under this stone!" Filled with compassion, he raised it up and immediately the Nine Demon Brothers escaped.

These Nine Demon Brothers reincarnated themselves into the nine sons of the king of Mongolia, Sogpo Jungkar. Soon their riches became immense and they decided to make war on Tibet.

At this same time, a monk from Lhasa, a *dobdob*, ignorant and rude, went to the monastery of Mindroling, to ask for alms there. He entered the courtyard while the lamas and the monks were conducting a particularly important ceremony, a very intricate ritual. The monks, furious at being disturbed, decided to punish the *dobdob* by beating him. However, the abbot of the monastery, Lama Terdaglingpa, who had the gift of foresight, told them: "Instead of beating the *dobdob*, you would do better to offer him a number of gifts, *tsampa*, a large amount of tea, both white and yellow butter, and spices. A time will come when he will be of great help to us." And eventually this *dobdob* was reincarnated as a Mongol war chieftain!

Meanwhile, the aggressive plans of the nine sons of the Mongol king became known to Lama Terdaglingpa. He then had a golden saddle fashioned, which was richly ornamented with turquoise and coral, and in the saddle he hid a written curse. Then he sent the saddle to the Mongol country, offering it for sale at a very high price so that only the king would be able to buy it. The nine sons would certainly covet it immediately!

The oldest son used this saddle during a race; he fell from the horse and died. The next day, the second son died in the same way. So it was with all the remaining seven others. The king then broke the saddle to pieces and found the curse!

He then set out against Tibet, pillaging and burning all the monasteries of the Nyingma sect, from the frontier to the doors of Lhasa.

One of the chieftains of the Mongol army was the reincarnated *dobdob*, and he refused to go to Mindroling, where he had received such a warm welcome in his previous life. And while approaching the monastery, his soldiers heard growls from the wooden tigers that adorn the door of the temple. Terrified, they fled.

Two butter lamps burn in front of the mummy of the Lama of Shang. Karma, finishing the story, recites *"Om mani padme hum"* in a voice more powerful than usual.

The Jewel

A good watchdog ought to have yellow hairs in its eyebrows;
The girl to marry ought to wear turquoise and coral.

In the morning, Sonam quickly prepares the temple of Trakyem
for the teaching of the "Union of the Three Precious Ones."[29]
He places the texts on a wooden support, underneath which
he has put a little barley. He hangs the large drum after tight-
ening the skins by placing the drum near the hearth for a few
minutes. Then, from a mixture of *tsampa*, water, butter, and red
color, he makes the *torma*, sacred figurines, in shape conical as
well as triangular, which represent the deities of the ritual.

The ceremony begins with the burning of juniper in front of
the temple. Tsultrim, a young devotee and nephew of Nyima
Tsering, blows three blasts on the conch, to signal the beginning of the prayers. The scripture of the "Union of the Three
Precious Ones" is always read three times, and tea is served to
those reciting the prayer by pilgrims throughout the ceremony.
During the interval between the readings, the pilgrims make
many hundreds of threefold prostrations. They rub prayer flags
on the volumes of the Kanjur and detach a small piece of the

ceremonial scarves that adorn the mummy of Shang Rinpoché. A woman asks for a little of the butter that ornaments the *torma*; this helps cure the skin diseases of the yaks.

Karma, slightly unwell, circumambulates the sanctuary while counting his rosary, and to count the rounds, each time he passes, he places a small pebble on a *chörten*. Knowing that Lama Tseyang, who has completed six months of a three-year retreat, is living in a cave near the temple, Karma, through the intermediary of the lama's attendant and with the presentation of a *khata*, asks for medication. The attendant comes back with a small cup filled with holy water, pills of long life, and the blessed scarf. Karma pours a little of the water in the hollow of his hand, some of this he drinks, then, with his wet palm, he moistens his forehead and head. He swallows one of the pills of long life and he puts the rest into his reliquary.

The first reading of the scripture is over and all the assistants drink the tea prepared by Norbu. We take the opportunity of the interval to leave for the nearby *gompa* of Nangkhung. This temple, set against a cliff, was built by Lama Jowo Ngawang Namgyal and is very old. It contains a large terracotta image of Padmasambhava and another of the founding lama. The upper story is a chapel, and the walls are covered with *tangkas* of Shakyamuni and of Prajnaparamita, the goddess of wisdom.

Back in Trakyem, the reading continues until the end of the afternoon. Gathering for the evening, we are many in the temple kitchen. There are people from Poldé, one of the villages of the Panzang valley, and some *drogpa*, originally from the land to the West called Hor, beyond Kang Tisé, now settled for more than ten years along the pastures of Panzang. They can be distinguished from the inhabitants of Dolpo by the way they keep their hair, which, made into in two plaits, falls on their shoulders.

In the temple kitchen on festival days, food is prepared for all the participants, who number at the very least one hundred.

The vessels for cooking rice and for churning tea are very large, and each temple is proud to have a tea churn that is large enough to provide tea for at least a hundred people!

The room is dimly lit with burning resinous slivers of pine. A fire of yak dung is kept going by Sonam, who tells the story of Nangsa. The audience has no difficulty in relating to this tale, although it concerns a far-off place.

Nangsa, a girl of great beauty, was chosen by the king to become his wife, even though she desired to devote herself to the Religion. Nangsa had to accept this.

Nangsa was all goodness and gentleness, but the king's sister was ill-natured and deceitful. The sister succeeded in convincing the king that Nangsa was wasting his wealth, when actually she was giving alms. Then, when Nangsa received a religious beggar, the sister accused her of adultery. The king, thinking Nangsa was unfaithful, and aided by his sister, beat her, leaving her for dead.

The body of Nangsa was exposed for seven days, but her soul meanwhile presented itself before the king of the Hells, who sent her back to earth, as her time of life was not yet completed.

On the seventh day the time came to burn the body. The "dead" raised herself and people cried out at this miracle. The king then permitted Nangsa to dedicate herself to a life of devotion and meditation, as she wished.

This narrative awakens in Karma the memory of another story with a theme of deceit and intrigue against the innocent and virtuous, and he proceeds to tell the following:

In the kingdom of the West, there was a king whose wise minister was pressing him to get married. The king had a divination made by an astrologer which revealed: "The king of a distant realm has two daughters, one of whom could become your wife. The elder is beautiful; she will give birth to an incarnation of Buddha Opamé. The younger is also beautiful; she will give birth to an incarnation of Buddha Chenrezi."[30]

The king asked for both of them in marriage. The elder gave birth to a son, Tondrup. Later, the younger sister also gave birth to a son, Chungdrung Yo. Then the elder queen died. The two boys were inseparable, and Chungdrung Yo always slept in the lap of his elder brother.

One day some children were playing near the palace, in view of the younger queen, and they built two thrones of stone, a large one for Tondrup, and a smaller one for Chung-drung Yo. They did this for each of the Four Directions.

The queen, taking this game as an omen, flew into a rage, thinking that the kingdom and the wealth would be for Tondrup, and that her son would have nothing.

A little later, the queen fell ill; no medicine, no ceremony of expiation was able to cure her. The king was in despair. The queen told him:

"Nothing can cure me; I am going to die."

"I will do anything to save you," said the king.

Quickly the queen said: "Take an oath on what you have just said."

And the king swore.

"Only the heart of your older son, Tondrup, can cure me," she said.

The king, horrified, refused at first, but as he had taken an oath, he had to comply. The king's minister warned Tondrup:

"You must flee from here, quickly. The young queen wishes you harm. I am going to give you a horse laden with food, and you must go."

Now Tondrup was holding Chungdrung Yo on his lap. He put him gently to the ground, but the child sensed that his elder brother was leaving him and he begged him so much that the two set off together.

The queen then hired a hunter and ordered him to kill Tondrup. But Tondrup was not to be found. The minister then advised the hunter to kill a goat and to bring the heart to the queen and to say that it was Tondrup's heart. This was done and the queen instantly recovered.

The two half-brothers wandered a great distance, but Tondrup had no water nor food for Chungdrung Yo, who died at the end of seven days. Tondrup, in despair, placed the body in a little cave and built a wall to protect it from wild animals. After this, he wandered aimlessly.

One day, attracted by the sound of cymbals, he came upon a hermit at his prayers.

"Who dares to come near me in my retreat?" the hermit demanded.

Tondrup explained the reason for his coming: "I am the son of a king, and I have been banished from my father's country by a jealous stepmother." At his request the hermit performed a divination according to which the two brothers would meet again after twenty years. Tondrup remained with the hermit as his attendant.

Now, the hermit was living in a land where the king possessed all kinds of wealth, except for a precious jewel that was guarded by the *lu*. The king said to his minister:

"I will give my daughter to the one who brings me the jewel."

The minister thought: "It is up to my son to find the jewel," and he went to consult with the hermit, who replied: "Only the son of a king can recover this jewel from the *lu* who guard it." The hermit was aware of the destiny of his own prince-attendant.

And, so, thanks to the hermit, Tondrup was able to retrieve the jewel and marry the king's daughter.

In the meantime, Chungdrung Yo was not really dead. Two birds fed him in the cave where Tondrup had put him: one gave him drink, the other food. Later, he lived amongst monkeys, feeding on the fruits of the forest; in the place of each fruit picked, another grew again.

Day after day, Chungdrung Yo called his elder brother: "*Ajo, Ajo!*"

At last, the two boys were reunited. They then returned to see their parents. The king had become old and sad, and the aged queen was filled with remorse.

Thus the older boy Tondrup had retrieved the jewel in the land of the hermit and had married the daughter of the king of that land. He became king there, and the younger brother Chungdrung Yo became king of the country of his birth.

How One Becomes Intelligent

He who knows the depth of the water can catch fish by the handful.

Everybody urges Karma to tell another story, and ignoring the late hour, Karma begins:

> Long ago in Tibet, a wise king had a son who was not very intelligent.
>
> "You are a young man without learning; you must learn how to be the chieftain of a kingdom; this you can learn through travel," said the father. "I am giving you three thousand gold coins and a servant to accompany you. You will learn, if you can, the rules of life and acquire the knowledge that a prince should have."
>
> The son left home, and travelling far, arrived at a pilgrim's shelter on the frontier of India. At night the servant, exhausted by the heavy load he carried, went to sleep. The boy, however, stayed awake and met a holy man who was chanting while accompanying himself on a one-stringed instrument.
>
> "Religious one, help me to gain intelligence," said the prince.
>
> "I will only bestow intelligence at the price of a thousand gold coins," the man replied.
>
> "I will give you one thousand gold coins; teach me," said the prince.

"Then hear my advice: In whatever situation you may find yourself, always act respectfully toward everyone and do not disparage anyone. People must never be treated contemptuously, whether they are powerful or seemingly insignificant. Remember that everyone is caught in the web of their karma," he told the boy, and he returned to his instrument.

The king's son was not satisfied by this. "Teach me more," he said.

"My teaching, whatever it may be, is worth a thousand gold coins," was the master's reply.

And the boy again gave a thousand gold coins. The master gave him this advice:

"In whatever situation you may find yourself, you must always help those who are in need. Do not turn away from an angry person, or someone in difficulty, but aid them and give them good advice." And again he took up his instrument.

However, the boy was not able to sleep. "Teach me more," he asked.

"Give me a thousand gold coins and I will tell you another wise word."

The boy gave the thousand gold coins that remained with him, and the master said:

"In whatever situation you may find yourself, always take the time to listen to the words of the lamas and the other wise people. And now this is my last word."

The following day, when the servant woke up, the bag with the gold coins was empty.

"What have you done with the gold coins?" he asked the prince.

"I have given them to a pious man who has taught me wisdom," replied the boy.

"What do we do now? I cannot remain a servant to a master who has no money," said the servant, and he left the prince.

The boy set off and, on the way, met one of his childhood playmates. He narrated his story, and added: "Not possessing anything, I have become a beggar. Now I cannot enter your house."

The boy's friend told him: "We have been friends for a long time; come in, everything here is yours, money, clothing, whatever I have."

"I am poor, I cannot stay," said the prince.

"I will give you all my wealth, my house, my fields," replied the friend, and he thought to himself: "Before, he was the son of a king; now what has happened to him!" And taking pity on his friend, he slid three gold coins into the prince's pocket without it being noticed.

The friend's house was like a palace. A rosary of pearls was hanging on the wall on which a deity with a peacock was painted.

Very early in the morning, the prince in meditation gazed at the peacock painted on the wall, and thought: "If I were a peacock I would be happy indeed." And he saw the painting come alive and the peacock swallow the pearls! The prince thought: "The peacock has swallowed the precious rosary. If I report this fact, no one will believe me; what am I going to say to my friend?"

And the prince fled; he went very far. The friend found neither the prince nor the rosary. "The king's son has gone," he declared. "He has carried off the rosary. He will have some difficulties. Where has he gone?" The prince arrived back in Tibet, a beggar, not having anything to eat. Someone gave him a little rice, and as he did not have a sack, he put it in his pocket and discovered the three gold coins. "These three gold coins belong to my friend. He will think that I have stolen not only the rosary, but also these coins!" he told himself.

He passed the night in the house of an old woman who proposed that he stay; he would take the place of a son. "In my turn, I will help you," she said. For a month, he lived with the old woman as if he were her son, and he gave her the three gold coins.

"Where did these three coins come from?" the old woman asked.

And the prince related the story of his life to the old woman.

"We must take care of these three gold coins," she said. She wrapped them in a *khata*.

In this land there was a king, and the prince's former servant had been able to enter unseen into the palace garden. During the night he stole fruit from the garden and during the day he hid in the trees, thus every day fruits were disappearing. The king and his minister were much puzzled by these happenings.

The king decided to personally watch over the garden, his sword and his dagger at his side, but he dozed off. The servant came silently down from the tree, took the sword and killed the king. Then, wearing the king's hat, he went to the minister to kill him also.

"Don't kill me!" said the minister. "You have killed the king and put on his hat; so I will recognize you as king. Take his wife and keep me as your minister." Thus the former servant of the prince became king.

However, at the end of two months, the time came when the king was due to present himself before his assembled subjects, at which time they had to pay homage to him. What could he do? He would be recognized as an imposter. So, the false king pretended to be ill and put off the date of the assembly.

Some months later, he made it known that he was cured, and announced to his subjects a distribution of tea, butter, and *tsampa*, as well as horse racing and archery competitions.

The old woman told the prince, "In seven days we must go to pay homage to the king. He will give tea, butter and *tsampa*."

The people of the kingdom came together for the announced festival. When the false king appeared, they said to themselves, "Oh, how the face of our king has changed; this must be due to his long illness." But the prince recognized his former servant, and thought to himself: "Oh, it is my servant! I am sure he has killed the king and thus acquired power. He is an imposter; I am going to denounce this evildoer." But, at the same time, he remembered the words of the holy lama: "In whatever situation you may find yourself, always act respectfully toward everyone and do not disparage anyone. People must never be treated contemptuously, whether they are powerful or seemingly insignificant. Remember that everyone is caught in the web of their karma." And accordingly he said nothing.

Two days later, the prince thought: "I must become the servant of this king!" He mentioned this to the old woman and eventually he was given the post of messenger in the palace.

Meanwhile, the queen, who did not like this king, became the mistress of the minister, and the prince-messenger discovered this.

One day, the queen became anxious: "The messenger has seen me with the minister. If the king learns of this, he will kill us! We must immediately get rid of this servant."

The queen wrote to a trustworthy friend: "Kill the one who brings you this message," and she had the letter carried by the prince.

On the way, the prince-messenger came across a little girl who was wearing a gold necklace and crying. He asked her the reason for her grief and she told him that her necklace had been adorned with a pearl which was lost when she slipped in the mud. The prince recalled the advice of the holy man: "In whatever situation you may find yourself, you must always help those who are in need. Do not turn away from an angry person, or someone in difficulty, but aid them and give them good advice." So the prince wanted to help the little girl find the pearl.

"While you look for the pearl, I am going to carry your message," said the girl.

The prince collected the mud from the road in a loosely woven sack. He then dipped the sack in the river—the soil all emptied out and the pearl remained behind in the sack. In this way he found the pearl. He replaced it in the necklace and waited for the little girl. Alas, she had delivered the message and immediately the friend of the queen had killed her.

The prince waited a whole day; the little girl did not come back. He went to look for her.

"What has happened to the little girl who carried the message?" he asked the queen's friend.

The friend replied: "The work is done."

"What have you done?" asked the prince-messenger.

"The message gave the order to kill her! I have killed her, as required," was the reply.

The prince thought: "I have just caused the death of a little girl, whom I did not even know, nor do I know her parents. What, then, is the teaching of the holy man worth?"

The queen thought: "The messenger is dead," but the next day, he was back at the palace.

The queen then sent a secret message to the oil-presser: "If anyone comes and asks you: 'Is the oil cooked?' throw that person immediately into the boiling oil." The queen had much power over her subjects.

Shortly after, she told the prince-messenger: "We need some oil; go to the oil-presser and ask: 'Is the oil cooked?' Go right away, and come back quickly."

The messenger left immediately.

On the road, he encountered a *lama-manipa* who was telling a religious story. The prince passed him by, but then he remembered what the pious lama had taught him: "In whatever situation you may find yourself, always take the time to listen to the words of the lamas and the other wise people." Accordingly, he retraced his footsteps and returned to the place where the *lama-manipa* was speaking. He passed the whole day near him.

But the queen, not having seen the messenger return, left on horseback to see the oil presser, and asked him: "Is the oil cooked?"

The presser seized the queen and threw her into the boiling oil.

The prince eventually left the *lama-manipa* and arrived at the presser's place. "Is the oil cooked?" he asked the presser.

"The oil is cooked and the work is finished," was the reply.

"What work are you speaking of?" asked the messenger.

"I have obeyed the queen's order to kill the first person who would come and say to me, 'Is the oil cooked?'" the presser told him.

The prince, realizing the danger which he had escaped, thought: "This pious one who instructed me is indeed a wise man!"

The king and the minister wondered about the absence of the queen. A search was made, but in vain. The minister said: "The messenger may know something about this."

So the messenger was questioned; the king recognized the prince and questioned him. The prince-messenger replied to each of them, saying: "I gave all my gold to a religious man who, three times, gave me advice: First, do not disparage anyone; second, help those in need; and third, listen to the holy words of wise men. Thus, I have not revealed your true identity at the time of the assembly of the people. Also, the queen was the minister's mistress; I knew this, but I said nothing. She wished to get rid of me, but caused a little girl to be killed before being killed herself by the oil-presser."

The king then said: "You are a good man, you are the son of my king. Before the day is over, you will be the king of this land. I will be your minister."

Thus, the prince became king of the land; the servant became his minister; the old woman lived in the palace, and the kingdom prospered.

The old woman reminded the king about the three gold coins he had been given by his friend: "Oh, I have forgotten my friend; I must return this money to him," said the prince-king. He sent his friend some fine horses and some jewels, then went to meet him.

"Why did you leave my house?" his friend asked.

The king said: "You had overwhelmed me with gifts, and without doubt, you thought that I was a thief because the pearl rosary disappeared. But it was the peacock painted on the wall that swallowed it!"

The friend said: "I have only thought about you as being in difficulty; I did not take you for a thief!"

The king offered a rosary of pearls and the three gold coins to his friend. At that moment, the peacock spat out the pearl rosary under the eyes of the two men!

The young king then said: "My father has acted wisely in requiring me to be educated," and he returned to his palace and to his father.

"Father, you did well to send me out to gain wisdom!"

The old king gave the insignia of his power to his son, a golden wheel, and thus he became a king, powerful and wise.

When finally we are stretched out in the temple for our second night, I ask Karma the meaning that he gives to the pilgrimage which we are making.

Does this question take him by surprise? He is beginning to become accustomed to some unusual questions. But he does not reply immediately, and then, not in the sense which I am prepared for:

"A pilgrimage results in an accumulation of merit; to accomplish this one must have a pure soul."
He is silent, then begins again:
"It is necessary to put an ivory ring on the left thumb. It is a remedy against all poisons, it protects against lightning, and it removes defilement."
And in spite of the late hour, he begins relating the "pilgrimage of pilgrimages," which he had made again and again: the one to the sacred Kang Tisé, also known as Kang Rinpoché, the axis of the world, known outside Tibet as Mount Kailash.

The Year of the Horse is devoted to the pilgrimage to Tso Mapam[31] and Kang Tisé, the two jewels of upper Tibet. One also benefits from this by making a visit to Purang and to the market of Gyanyima, close to the Indian border. Yaks are loaded with wool and dried cheese. They return with cotton, sugar, both white and raw, tea balls, and cups and bowls of turned wood from the country of Limi. The route itself is very long and one must pay careful attention while crossing the rivers, for the currents are always strong.

Six years ago, we made the pilgrimage of Kang Tisé with a group of friends. We arrived at Tarchen, at the base of Kang Tisé, in time for the full moon of the Fourth Month, the first day of the pilgrimage season when the large pole for prayer flags is raised.

The first stop on the *nékhor* of Kang Tisé is at Chöku Gompa. Here pilgrims take imprints of the hands of the image in the temple and drink a little tea. Then we descend into a valley where two pure currents of water meet: one of a stream, and the other from a source that emerges from beneath a huge rock. After a halt at a place where women desiring a child stop to make a vow, we go up to the temple of Dirapug, to honor the imprints of a sacred *dri* which once bedded down there. Higher up, we reach the rock face known as Trinchen Pami Tinlé. On the face of that rock, at shoulder height, is a small cavity in the surface of the rock. One must stand seven steps back from the rock and perform three prostrations. Then, with the eyes well closed, with the arm raised in front and the index finger extended forward, one advances toward the rock. One hopes that one's extended index finger is able to find and enter the cavity in one attempt! If one is successful, all sins are forgiven.

Nearby is a rock called "White and black sins." Another method of purifying oneself is to squeeze through the very narrow opening in the rock.

At the pass of Drolma, there is a small platform. There one puts some hair, old clothes, or a little blood, and all the evil influences that have become attached to one will remain there. There, we would eat a little sugar, and one of our companions would recite a prayer.

On the way back to Dolpo, we again see the Tso Kawa, imprints left by holy lamas, and shrines.

The pilgrimage of Kang Tisé removes all sins.

After a silence, Karma adds: "If, in the same year, one is able to pay one's respects to the three Jowo at Lhasa, at Purang, and at Kyirong, this is indeed perfection for the pilgrim!"

The Man of Evil Ways
and the Man of Good Ways

The man who speaks rudely is chased away;
Dogs are unleashed against the man who is in rags.

A heavy hailstorm bursts the moment we leave Trakyem.

The lama *sera shungkhen* of Saldang is certainly very busy! It is he who has the gift of stopping hail by his magic powers. We had met him on the way up to Trakyem. He lives in a small house above the village. It differs from the others by the large number of stones carved with *mantras* which are piled up along the walls, and by an exterior incense burner which is a square-shaped stone construction, surmounted by an old earthen cooking pot in which juniper branches are burnt.

We take the lower or valley trail. Not far off the trail, five generations ago, lived a hermit who belonged to the despised social status of the blacksmiths. During his lifetime, the villagers refused him all rights to religious practice, but when he died and when the body was cremated, it was seen that the letters "Ah" and "Om" were engraved on his bones, which is considered a sign of saintliness.

By the Namgung River are the ruins of two hermitages; on the right bank stand the ruins of the hermitage of Rimkhang, and on the left bank are those of the hermitage of Rimdzong. Sonam had told us the story of these two hermitages where long ago two lama-magicians of exceptional power fought each other, each using his magic powers. Each of them believed he possessed the greater powers. The lama-magician of Rimkhang sent his adversary a plate of *tsampa*. No sooner did the magician of Rimdzong touch it, than he lost an eye! The magician of Rimdzong avenged himself by releasing a dog that rapidly changed into a tiger, causing such terror to his enemy that he died of fright.

We are soaked to the skin and decide to halt again at Nyima Tsering's house at Saldang.

Some yaks which have just returned from the valley of Para are tied up in the courtyard in front of the house. They are still loaded. Their packs carry grain, maize flour and various objects of wood: containers for water, tea churns, and bundles of pine slivers. The slivers are formed of particularly resinous pinewood, cut from the base of large living trees, and are used for illuminating the house at night.

Up on the first floor of the house, the lama *tulku* of Dechen Labrang is occupied with painting a wooden support for a new prayer-wheel, while a servant is busy cutting up the strips of printed paper carrying the mantra *Om Ah Hum Bendza Guru Pema Siddhi Hum*[32] that will be placed inside the prayer-wheel. The chapel of the house is a large room of more than twenty square meters. Against one wall, a row of shelves holds the religious items: images, books, reliquaries, and vases for holy water. Some *tangkas* are hung on the other walls, and among them is a large printed calendar of the type common today in India, in vivid colors, adorned with Hindu deities.

The chapel serves also as a store for fabric, saddles, pack-saddles for yaks, and saddle carpets. On the side of the room with a single window, the carpenter of Saldang is building the frame that will support the new prayer-wheel. The lower axle extends to form a crank to which a rope will be tied so that Nyima Tsering will be able to spin the wheel by pulling on the rope. In this way he will be able to activate the prayer-wheel while stretched out on a bed by the window. This window, of which the upper part is in the shape of a lotus petal, looks out over the courtyard. One can well imagine the master of the house spying on the life of the household, all the while praying a little, mechanically!

In the courtyard, the leader yak keeps himself aloof from the others. He is decorated with the ornaments associated with his function: a collar with three red dyed yak tails and a small bell, and two more bells fixed on a strap at the height of the shoulders. Attached to the load is a little vertical rod carrying a prayer flag; the horns are coated with ochre.

The loads of the yaks are now examined, one by one, because the caravan has also been through the hailstorm. The moist grain is spread out on canvases, the ropes and straps are put out to dry. The rice beer prepared for the return of the caravaneers is offered all around. "Rice beer releases the tongue and opens the heart," says one of the men. The personality of Nyima Tsering has surprised us, and we discuss this at night during our meal. Karma, who has heard much about him in Changtang, said he is very hard to deal with. His piety appears a little ostentatious and the offerings he describes as being his were, in reality, not only his, but also from the other members of the community. Karma appears to be reflecting upon our observations as he relates to us the following story:

A long time ago, two men, one sharp-witted and deceitful, the other less clever but honest, became friends.

"Now we are friends," said the deceitful one. "Let us go together on a trip and do some trading."

The two men set out right away. They made a lot of money and returned to their country. The cunning one then said, "This money should not be brought to our homes, as all our relatives would then want a portion of it, and we would have to share it among many."

So they agreed to hide the gold and silver in the hollow trunk of a tree whose location they alone knew.

"Later, when we have need of money, we both will come and take some, but it is necessary that we come together," they agreed.

One day, however, the deceitful one went there alone and carried away the entire treasure. Then, a little later, the two of them visited the tree, and not finding the treasure, the deceitful one immediately accused his friend: "We had hidden money in this tree; we are the only ones to know this, I have not taken it; therefore, you are the thief!"

The simple soul swore that he had not stolen it and the other then said: "In this tree, there is a divinity. Let us find a judge to ask this divinity who has stolen our treasure."

The deceitful one had earlier discussed all of this with his father, who had agreed to hide himself in the tree, and he instructed his father in this way: "A judge will come and ask: 'O divinity, who has stolen the treasure?' You will reply: 'The simple soul has taken the money.'"

When the judge arrived to settle the dispute the deceitful one proposed to ask the help of the divinity in the tree. Then the question was put: "Divinity in this tree, will you name the thief?"

"The thief is the simple man," said a voice in the tree.

"This divinity is a fraud!" the simple one said. "Make a fire at the base of the tree, and we will know the truth!"

The judge lit a fire and an angry voice was heard in the tree: "You have wanted to be more clever than the others and you have smoked out your father!"

Once more Karma speaks:

A long time ago, two men were living in Tibet: one, known as Semba Chungchung,[33] was full of goodness, thinking only of doing good. The other, Hampa Chenpo,[34] was crafty and ill-natured.

Semba Chungchung supported his very large family, which consisted of his wife, ten young children, his father and his mother. Every day, he went to the summit of the mountain to gather an armful of flowers which he would sell. In this way he collected enough money to be able to feed his family.

Hampa Chenpo was living by various expedients, stealing and borrowing money and never paying it back.

One day, Hampa Chenpo asked Semba Chungchung what he lived on. "I gather an armful of flowers every day, and I go to sell them," he replied.

"I know where there are flowers in quantity, come with me," Hampa Chenpo told him.

They arrived at the edge of a cliff under which flowed a river; halfway down the cliff was a cave where flowers were growing in great numbers.

"Go down by this rope, cut the flowers and prepare the bunches," Hampa Chenpo told him. "I will raise up the loads gradually, as the work goes on."

Semba Chungchung began to work, preparing a number of loads and attaching them to the rope. But then, just when he wanted to leave, he discovered that the rope was no longer there. Hampa Chenpo had gone off, taking the rope and abandoning him. Semba Chungchung made all kinds of prayers; nothing came of them.

Sometime later, Hampa Chenpo, thinking his companion was dead, went to Semba Chungchung's family. The parents and children, convinced by him that Semba Chungchung had died, became his servants and he took Semba Chungchung's wife for himself.

Semba Chungchung ate grass and flowers and was confined to the cave for six months by the impassable river. Finally winter came and, the river having frozen over, he could cross over and go back home. Semba Chungchung reentered his house, but found nobody there. So he set out to wander through the world.

One day, he stopped in a temple dedicated to Ling Gesar, the divine hero, and settled down to sleep.

In the middle of the night, a tiger entered the temple. The tiger was a servant of Ling Gesar. Semba Chungchung, terrified, hid himself behind the door. Then the image of Gesar began to speak!

"Uncle Tiger, you have come!"

Then a leopard entered.

"Uncle Leopard, you have come!"

And then a bear arrived.

"Uncle Bear, you have come!"

Then Gesar asked the tiger:

"What is the news from the land of China?"

"The emperor suffers with his eyes, and no remedy is able to cure him. How can his illness be relieved?"

"A needle has been left in the eye of a dragon embroidered on a silk flag. The dragon is the emperor's protector and the needle has offended him," said Gesar.

The leopard then said:

"At the center of the land of China, there is a beautiful girl, but she does not speak, and she does not have a son. This girl, how can she regain her speech?"

"At the summit of a mountain is a medicinal flower. In the morning a little dew lies on this flower; it is necessary to drink some of this water in order to regain speech," said Gesar.

The bear in his turn, said:

"In the country of China, in the region of the north, a great drought is raging; for three years there has been no harvest. How can water be made to come?"

"In the middle of the plain, there is a tree. A snake is trapped under the roots. If it is freed, water will be plentiful," said Gesar.

Hidden at the back of the temple, nearly dead from fear, Semba Chungchung had heard all these words; then the animals left.

Semba Chungchung set out for China, and along the way he heard it said that the emperor was suffering. He went to the palace and presented himself as a healer. He said to the emperor:

"Behind you, there is a flag and the dragon that is embroidered on it suffers because a needle was forgotten in its eye!"

The emperor took a look, withdrew the needle from the eye of the dragon, and was instantly cured!

"I have offered a thousand rituals, invited many lamas, nothing came of it! As for you, you come and you cure me! You are a saintly lama; I give you, as promised, half of my wealth and since your wisdom is so great, I request you to cure my daughter."

Semba Chungchung, recalling the words of Ling Gesar, made his way toward the mountain top. For a month, each morning he collected the dew from the medicinal flower. He then offered the pure dew to the daughter of the emperor; she drank it and immediately began to speak.

The emperor thanked him again, and asked him to help in a region where, for more than three years, nothing grew because of a severe drought. The rivers were dry, and people and animals had died by the thousands. Semba Chungchung set out alone and went to the vast plain. He found there a sandalwood tree under which a snake was trapped. He made an offering and freed the snake. Immediately, a spring burst forth, then transformed itself into a river. The land became prosperous again and the inhabitants wanted Semba Chungchung to become their king.

But Semba Chungchung had only one thought: to find his family and his parents. So he went off to Tibet with a band of warriors. Along the way, he met Hampa Chenpo, who was astonished to see that his companion had become a powerful chieftain. Hampa Chenpo asked Semba Chungchung what he had done to acquire such great power?

Semba Chungchung innocently related his entire adventure: the night in the temple of Ling Gesar, the healing of the king, the healing of the girl, and finally the restoration of fertility to the plain.

Hampa Chenpo, full of envy, went to spend a night in the temple. The tiger, then the leopard, and finally the bear arrived.

Ling Gesar asked:

"What news do you bring me from the land of China?"

"The emperor is cured; he does not suffer any more in his eye," said the tiger.

"The girl speaks very well now," said the leopard.

"The desert-like land has recovered its fertility," said the bear.

"But how is it that all these troubles were cured?" asked all the animals.

"A man was hidden behind the door of the temple and overheard my words," said Ling Gesar.

Fear seized Hampa Chenpo. He made a little sound, and the three animals found him and devoured him.

So, Semba Chungchung became a powerful chieftain, always engaged in good works.

In the night, Norbu wakes up. A mouse has made a hole in the sack of *tsampa* bought from Nyima Tsering, which Norbu is also using as a pillow. Mending the hole, he angrily says, "Not only are we given coarse *tsampa* to eat, but it has been eaten up by the proprietor's mice instead of by us!"

The Horseman
Who Does Not Steal or Lie

Malicious words will not be listened to;
Virtuous words will be on everyone's lips.

An old woman from Karang comes to Nyima Tsering's house at dawn, waking up the house. Leaning on her staff, she cries: "Last night, the lama of Karang hit me with a hoe; he says I exceeded my share of water from the canal, but my share of water was the correct amount."

Nyima Tsering's face shows a closed mind. He sends the woman back with some harsh words, "The assembly of Karang will decide!"

This event causes a memory to return: some years ago, one of Nyima Tsering's sons crippled a villager of Saldang over the same issue: a stolen share of water.

We resume our pilgrimage. It is a good day's journey from Saldang to Koma, our next stop. After fording the Nangkhong River, we climb up to the pass of She. From the pass, one sees the houses of Koma scattered in the fields of barley and mustard, then some *chörten* and a large water reservoir.

In the small valley just below the pass is a large black tent, and some mastiffs run toward us menacingly. Reaching Koma, we find hospitality. Our hostess, a very good-natured woman, tells us: "Koma was a large village. It used to be a place loved by the divinities until there was a conflict between two lamas, one in Tibet, the other at Lo. They fought each other by casting spells and by evil charms. The Lama of Lo made his way, exhausted, to Koma, and died here. Since that day, the land has become barren, the grass has no vigor, water is scarce, and we have to store it during the night in a reservoir. We draw our shares of water by lot, and there are always disputes!"

Our hostess is looking after a newly born grandchild who sleeps in a basket, deep in a bag filled with crushed dry goat dung. The child's head is covered with a cotton bonnet adorned with cowries. The cowries have a purpose: when the infant sleeps, his soul leaves the body and wanders, and it so happens that the soul is sometimes chased by a demon; if it does not have enough time to reenter the infant's body, the soul can take refuge in one of the shells.

We spend the evening speaking of pilgrimages. The whole family has made the great round through Kathmandu in the Year of the Bird.[35] The old woman remembers the names of all the innkeepers along the way. Leaving Panzang, they had passed through *drogpa* country to Shungru, then to Bawa, then to Kyirong to worship the image of the Jowo; then to Kathmandu where it took fifteen days to visit all the sanctuaries. They returned by the valley of the Kali Gandaki.

While describing the pilgrimage, our hostess lists the temples they visited in the valley of Kathmandu. There are many legends concerning these sacred places. Karma contributes details on the origin of the Seven Giants, defenders of the Religion, who now reside in the Changtang:

> A long time ago, a very wealthy family named Utpal lived in the valley of Kathmandu. One son became a monk and stayed a very long time in meditation. Everyone knew this recluse and his spiritual attainments.

One day, the queen of Li-yul went to the bank of the Bagmati River to bathe. A large snake who was sleeping at the edge of the water began to follow her. The hermit, meditating nearby, saw the snake and the danger to the queen. He decided to break his meditation and warn her. He ran toward her to warn of the danger.

The queen saw the hermit running toward her, but did not see the snake, and she thought: "This man has evil intentions; he wants to ravish me." The hermit tried to warn the queen, and shouted: "Watch out, Queen of Li-yul, a snake is following you!" But, frightened, the queen threw herself from the height of a large rock into the river and was drowned. Terrified, the hermit ran away.

Witnesses of the scene had not seen the snake, and reported the event to the king, who decided to seize the hermit so that he could be put to death. He sent his soldiers to the Four Directions in search of the fugitive, who had taken the road to Tibet. The hermit took refuge at Rum-né at the base of a large rock. There, the soldiers found him and killed him.

The soul of the hermit did not find peace, and his blood produced seven eggs. The eggs swelled and seven men came out of them, resembling demons, the Rolwa Gyabdün, who, like so many demons, had very great power. They met Urgyen Rinpoché, who gave them religious initiation and transformed them into Defenders of the Religion. They are now protecting the pastures in the Changtang.

At the request of his audience, Karma begins another story:

In times of old in Tibet, there were two kings. Shar Toyö Trulwa, the king of the East, passionately coveted the realm of Nub Nyima Gyaltsen, the king of the West, who was virtuous and wise. The king of the East had three daughters; the king of the West had a virtuous horseman called "Horseman who does not steal or lie."

One day, the king of the East provoked the king of the West, expressing doubt about the virtue of the horseman. "If the horseman never steals, it will surely happen that he will lie!"

The king of the West defended the horseman and proposed putting him to a test. "If the horseman lies, I will give you my kingdom. If he does not lie, I will take possession of yours," said the king of the West.

Not far from the boundary of the two kingdoms, the horseman watched over the divine horse of the king of the West. This horse had flanks the color of the inside of a conch.

The king of the East told his daughters of his intention to test the horseman. They decided to help their father.

The eldest daughter approached the horseman. "Horseman of a thousand virtues, I wish to become your wife," she said.

"I do not desire you. I am only a simple servant of the king of the West," he replied.

The girl, going back to the palace, related what had happened and the reason the horseman refused.

The next day, the king of the East sent his second daughter. She, too, was refused.

The third daughter tried in turn. She pleaded with the horseman to let her stay near his tent. Touched by her firm resolve, he took her as his wife.

One day, some time later, the girl appeared to fall gravely ill; she applied red ochre to her right nostril and her upper lip.

"I am very ill," she told the horseman.

"What must we do to cure you?" he asked.

"No remedy can save me, I am going to die."

"Isn't there some means of curing this illness? I will do anything to save you!" he told her.

"The only effective remedy is a little blood from the heart of Lharta Shelgichörten, the divine horse," she said.

"But this is the divine horse of the king of the West! How can you ask such a thing!"

"Then I am going to die," said the king's daughter, and her condition became worse.

The horseman reflected for a long time. Finally he decided to save the girl and to kill the horse. He took a little blood from the heart and it cured her in no time!

The daughter then decided to visit her father. The horseman hesitated to announce the divine horse's death.

On the boundary of the two kingdoms the horseman made two *towos*. On the side of the king of the West he constructed a *towo* of white stones and on the side of the king of the East he did the same with black stones. First, facing the white *towo*, he made three prostrations, saying, "If the *towo* collapses by itself, I may lie to my master!" but the *towo* remained erect. Then turning to the black *towo*, he made three prostrations and said, "May the *towo* collapse if I must tell the truth." The black *towo* collapsed.

Anxious, but resolved not to lie, the horseman went to his master. The two kings were together, aware of the arrival of the horseman. At the intersection of the roads of the East and the West, they were seated in a tent. The horseman appeared before them, alone.

The king of the East was convinced that the horseman was going to lie.

The king of the West inquired:

"Horseman who does not steal or lie, have you truly arrived? The divine horse, is it in good health?"

"O king, my master, I have killed the splendid horse."

"Why have you killed it?" demanded his master.

"The three daughters of the king of the East came to see me in the pasture; the third stayed with me. She fell ill, and to save her, I have, at her request, killed the splendid horse. I preferred to save a human life by the death of the horse which was an animal."

Thus, the horseman had not told a lie. The king of the East lost his wager and his kingdom, which the king of the West gave to the faithful horseman.

How to Rid Oneself of a Rival

If a wolf runs too much, its skin will become loose on its body;
If a bird hops about too much, it will break its feet.

A very violent storm breaks over Koma in the middle of the night; the rain water spreads across the roof terrace where we are sleeping and we get soaked. Early in the morning, our hostess lights the fire; she prepares a broth, a mixture of *tsampa*, dried cheese and sheep fat. As an auspicious gift, she offers us several measures of wheat flour, a rarity in Dolpo.

A half day's walk separates Koma from Shimen, which is situated on the north bank of the Panzang River. During a rest stop, we dry in the sun the clothes which were soaked during the night.

At Shimen the mustard is in flower, and the fields, a rich yellow-gold, contrast with the surrounding bare slopes. Here Karma has a friend named Kansom, who is his host at the time of the annual barter of salt and grain. Kansom offers us hospitality and asks us a thousand questions, all the while spinning a rope of yak hair. His house is squalid. He takes a battered pot covered with a thick layer of soot and heats water for tea. After churning, the tea is heated in an earthen pot which appears not to have been used for ages.

Kansom speaks of the terrible winter he has just survived. He lost five yaks and was obliged to replace them at the buying rate of a hundred and fifty rupees per yak.

Kansom is preoccupied with the annual bartering. Normally, people from Jumlang come as far as Shimen by the end of the Fifth Month, with their loads of rice and dried chillies that they barter for salt, wool and mastiff puppies. They also exchange, by equal weight, wool for honey, an item very much appreciated in Dolpo for its medicinal properties. But this season people have not yet come from Jumlang. Up until last year, one could obtain in Tibet two measures of salt for one measure of barley. This year the *drogpa* take two measures of barley for only three measures of salt. Listening to Kansom, one could assume that he will be well enough informed so that he does not lose anything at the time of the next barter.

Shimen and Tingkyu, our next halt, control the passes that give access to the pastures and to the salt lakes of Tibet. The villagers benefit from their proximity to these resources. Karma has met them all at the time of trading and knows the number of yak loads they trade each year.

In winter, salt replaces water in the seven ritual bowls that are placed on the altar. It is collected on the shore of lake Trabyé Tsakha in the Changtang, which is fifteen days' walk to the north from Dolpo. The divine guardian of the salt is Trabyé Apa Gyalpo, who zealously watches over this treasure of the *lu*. At the center of the lake is a large rock, the home of the Protector, a white sheep. To approach this holy place, one must have a pure heart, make an incense offering and hoist a pole with a flag of five colors on the top of the pass that overlooks the lake; then snap the sling with "nine eyes."

We talk of the nomadic life of the *drogpa*, divided between the care of his flock and the search for pasture, especially in the winter, when forage is scarce.

"In *drogpa* country, the men have the responsibility of the herds of yaks and are also occupied in trade, so they can be absent from the tent for long periods," says Karma.

There was a *drogpa* family in the Changtang. While the husband was away tending the herd, the wife had a lover who stayed in the tent.

The wife said to the lover, "One day, I will go with my husband to the pasture and you will come there and kill him!"

However, the husband, who had left at dawn, had returned without warning to keep an eye on the lovers; so he was able to overhear their words.

In the herd that he was grazing, there was a black sheep which he killed. He buried the skin of the animal, washed the entrails and filled them with sugar and sweet syrup, then he cooked them. The lover arrived, armed with a long sword, and the husband sat down and began to eat the entrails. They smelled good and the lover asked:

"What is this meat that has such a good aroma?"

"It is a sausage made with human flesh," was the reply.

"You eat human flesh?"

"Human entrails are delicious. Here, taste them."

The lover tasted them, found the taste very good, and asked for more.

"You have, then, killed a man in order to have his intestines?"

"It's my wife who gave them to me!" replied the husband.

"Your wife, then, has killed a man?" demanded the lover, a little anxiously.

"My wife knows how to draw out the intestines from a man without killing him."

"How does she do it?"

"She begins to caress the man from the head to the lower back and takes the intestines out from behind."

The lover, having come to kill his rival, left, wondering about this woman who was perhaps a demoness!

Meanwhile, the husband returned to their tent.

The woman had been thinking, "My husband is dead; I am going to be able to live with my lover peacefully and undisturbed." Night came and to her great astonishment the husband returned. He ate some *tsampa* with a fine appetite and drank some tea.

"Did not a man come to see you this morning?" she asked.

"Actually, a man did come to see me, armed with a splendid sword. I think he was a deity."

"Why do you say that?"

"This man hid under his hair a flat cap of turquoise and from his lower back he had a tail of conch."

The wife thought, "This cap of turquoise and this tail of conch shell shows that he is indeed a deity!"

The next day, the husband decided to absent himself for several days in order to do some trading. The lover, therefore, set himself up in the tent. In the middle of the night, the woman wanted to verify the existence of the cap of turquoise and the tail of conch shell. She passed her hand softly on the head and down the back of the lover. He, awakening, and remembering the description of the extraction of intestines, fled in haste.

Thus the husband returned and resumed living with his wife, in peace and quiet.

The Child and the Demoness

When two lamas cast spells, the demons themselves run away.

Kansom, our host in Shimen, is preoccupied by his loss of animals during the past winter and laments: "We do not have a *lhapa*, a medium, in Dolpo. You in *drogpa* country at least have this resource to help with looking after the herds, to protect them with magic spells."

"Actually," says Karma, "lamas do not have any power over the illnesses of animals. They supply protective charms, but when something disastrous happens, there is nothing they can do. At Shungru, we have a *pachen*, a soothsayer, who fights the most serious illness of yaks and sheep. He knows how to limit the mischief of the *tsen* and, most importantly, how to overwhelm the evil power of a *dümo*, a demoness, as they are very common in *drogpa* country, where they haunt the herders' encampments.

One day, two hunters went off and killed a *kyang*, a wild ass. Back at the camp, the son of one of the hunters, six years old, was guarding the tent. A *dümo* stole the child and carried it off, far away. She lived in a tent around which there were piles of dead men and horses.

At dawn, the demoness went off in search of food. At the same time, the hunters were searching for the child. They went into the demoness' tent, where the fire had died out. The child, tied up behind a trunk, called out to his father: "Father, I am the prisoner of a wicked demoness, don't stay here, she will kill you; but after two days, send our cow, Ba tratatrari, and see that she touches the stays of the tent."

The hunters, following the child's advice, returned to their encampment.

The demoness returned that night, carrying on her back three bodies: those of a man, a horse, and a wild yak.

This demoness was frightening to look at, with her four copper teeth, two above, two below. She would go out for water, taking with her a leather container made from the stomach of a sheep. One day, the child inflated the container and pierced it in many places with a needle so that the water leaked out of it as fast as it was filled. The demoness pulled out a tooth and a hair of her moustache and made a knot at the place of each hole. Thus she had to pull out all her hairs and all her teeth.

The demoness possessed a special copper needle. Whatever happened to the needle happened to her. If the needle was safe, the demoness could not be harmed. If the needle was bent in one direction, the demoness' body would bend in the same direction; if it was bent in another direction, the demoness' body would bend in the other direction; and if the needle was to break, the demoness would die. This needle was her *sog-kyob*, her life support.

Two days after the father's visit, the cow arrived, and it made a stay of the tent vibrate. The demoness was asleep, tired out. The child, hearing the sound, came out and climbed up on the cow, taking with him the demoness' needle.

The demoness, seeing the child escape, threw her right breast over her left shoulder, and her left breast over the right shoulder, and began to run after the child, with blood filling her terrible mouth. The child, seeing that he was being pursued, took hold of the demoness' needle and bent it as much as he could. Immediately the demoness bent over too, her head touching her feet. The child arrived near his home and straightened the needle; the demoness immediately straightened herself, shouting: *"To-u trug mug tug to to."* The child again bent the needle, this time in the other direction, and the demoness' head went back and her neck touched her heels. Thus the child was able to reach home.

"Father, I have succeeded in stealing the demoness' needle, her life support!"

The father tried to break the needle with a big stone; he finally managed with the help of an iron hammer. Thus the demoness, whose life was linked with this magic needle, died.

The child was very wise and possessed supernatural gifts. In fact, many people before him had tried to destroy the demoness, but without success. The *drogpa* gave the child the name of Norbu Tramdu. As his parents were poor, he plucked some cow's hairs; the white hairs became white sheep; the black hairs became yaks; and the motley hairs became horses.

Thus he gained a fortune and everyone's respect.

Then Karma adds: "There are always demons who bring on a curse! In the province of Tsang, tradition requires that the girl who is going to be married should be carried off by the groom's friends and that the girl's relations resist this kidnapping by all kinds of tricks."

Two rich families had decided to unite their children. The night of the ceremony, the girl disappeared. The boy's parents thought that she had stayed at home, but the parents of the girl alleged that she had been kidnapped by her future husband.

Actually, it was a demon that had taken human form and had carried her off to make her his wife. The family searched in vain. She reappeared on the seventh day. The marriage then took place, and the girl eventually gave birth to a very handsome child. At one month, he appeared to be six months old; at one year, he appeared to be three. He had all the gifts: excellence in archery and firearms, he was the strongest in war games, but he did not want to know anything about the Religion. This child came to be known as Tsangpa Dretrug.

When he became chieftain of the country, he persecuted all the lamas. A *ngagpa*, a lama-magician, who tired of this, made a divination and discovered the chieftain's true nature. It was decided to do away with him.

The *ngagpa* made an image of Tsangpa Dretrug. He put the image on nine carpets piled one atop the other, and placed a table of offerings before it. He worshipped the effigy day after day, removing a carpet each day. The ninth day, when he removed the last carpet, Tsangpa Dretrug died. The magic was powerful and the Religion was restored to its glory. The lama-magician was an incarnation of the Buddha.

Tashi Taken, the Gelder

When the rider dreams of going to a thousand different places, the horse under him gets tired.

From Shimen to Tingkyu, the trail follows the gorge of the Panzang Chu. Here the gorge is so narrow that the sun's rays reach the ground only during the summer. We pass by some fallow terraces, then the ruins of the village of Pal, and the ruins of the temple of Ragar Khang. Further along, an entrance-*chörten* marks another abandoned settlement.

A man walking toward us is recognized by Karma; it's Tashi Taken, the gelder. Tashi is in the mood to talk.

We all sit down beside the trail and Karma relates the news from Shey and Nangkhong. Tashi, in turn, is returning from Tingkyu where he had gone to collect payment for a gelding he had done two months earlier. He received a measure of barley, a measure of butter, a new rope, a felt cover, a one-year-old sheep, and a ceremonial scarf.

"How does one castrate a stallion?" I ask.

"In the Third Month, when the Six Stars[36] disappear from the evening sky; that's the good time. The animal is placed on his back in a little trench, with his legs tied. A blanket of white felt is placed under his head. The owner puts a bit of butter on each ear as a token of good fortune. Some helpers hold the head and the tail. While the tongs become red in the fire, with a knife I cut the skin of the sack and I pull out the testicles, pressing the skin down, while reciting: 'Little white vein, little red vein of the belly, little white fast vein, have pity.'

"I pass the blade of the knife slowly between the veins, then cut the ligaments with the red hot tongs. I throw the testicles some distance, saying:

> May the birds take them away,
> May the dogs take them away.

"Then I clean the tongs, reciting a prayer to my protective deity. I put bits of butter in the middle of the forehead and on the ears of the horse, and I give him a new name like Samlep ('One who arrives immediately where he wants to').

"The horse suffers. After he is released, he rolls to the right and to the left. Then he must be well fed each night with barley and beer. On the seventh day, the wound is washed, and he is ridden without a saddle. The saddle is used only when the wound has healed."

Tashi reminds me of Kunchog Gyaltsen, the smith of Tarap. He shares a similar physique and a similar bent of mind, a broad knowledge of things which possess a somewhat mysterious nature. Perhaps the fact that both these men are able to handle red hot iron without burning themselves also gives them something of the spirit in common?

Tashi comments on the recent loss of a horse at Shimen: "It was a gelding with a white coat, the ears were always pricked and he had three tufts of hair, *norbu pun sum*, on the forehead, the hair soft as the down of a bird."

Karma mentions a horse he used to have, sired by a wild stallion on the northern plain. "But no horse can equal Tawo Kyango Yarwa of the hero Gesar or Goma Dralang Drogyog of Yoklari, or Lharta Karchen of Takar Mikar!" he says.

We part company and resume our separate ways. After a further four hours' walk, the valley widens out, becoming a broad cultivated area. Tingkyu, worthy of its name of "plain," is located in this spacious valley, more than three kilometers wide. The group of houses is dominated by the ruins of a square tower.

We pass through the village to go to the temple of Tralung, which is situated some two hundred meters above the valley floor. Near the temple, the odor of alcohol drifts in the air. Wrinkling his nose, Karma says:

At the *gompa* of Dorjé Trag[37]
The religious practice is not good.
From the chimney hole
Fall drops of barley beer.

And, in fact, Lama Karma Tsegya, the owner of the *gompa*, is in the process of distilling barley beer to prepare *arag*.

The temple of Tralung is built to a square plan, with a porch. The lintel over the porch is supported by artfully carved lion heads. The interior is painted and many *thangkas* hang on the walls.

Lama Karma Tsegya, born in the province of Kham, is a renowned painter. He teaches painting as well as rituals to the religious young of Dolpo. The first steps of instruction last from six months to a year. An apprentice lives with his master; he provides his own food, and offers a contribution in kind (*tsampa*, butter, meat, wool) in payment for the lessons.

The Battle of Gesar
and the Demon Akyung

A man who talks with the right words is wise;
A piece of straight wood makes a good beam for scales.

Lama Karma Tsegya reminds me a little of Marpa, the teacher of
Milarepa, by his tall and powerful stature and his simple and
direct approach. His rough manners belie the delicacy with which
he paints *tangkas*. At the moment he is almost drunk. He insists
that we drink, and makes fun of us and of our pilgrimage.

One of the sons of Tsering Puntsog of Tarap is learning to paint
in Tralung. He is at work drawing *Dra-lha*, the deity "Protecting
from the Enemies" that one associates with the Nyingma sect.

As we sip our *arag*, Karma, who has heard this epic countless times, refreshes our memories of the encounter of the young
Gesar and the demon Akyung:

> Gesar, the "Little Man from Tibet," fought the demon
> Akyung.
> Riding his horse, Tawo Kyango Yarwa, Gesar came to a
> gloomy land with a dark sky. He then arrived at the home
> of the demon and met the demon's wife, Bagsa Bumdé, a

demoness. Bagsa Bumdé was a grotesque creature who had only two teeth, an incisor of copper and one of iron. "I smell the Little Man of Tibet," she said. Gesar aimed an arrow at a fingernail of the demoness; she saw a flame burst forth and became afraid: "Don't draw your bow, come in. What brings you here?" she asked. "I have come to kill Dü Akyung!" "He has gone off toward the mountain in the north. If I help you to kill him, will you stay with me?" Gesar accepted the proposal.

In the late afternoon, Dü Akyung returned, and the demoness hid Gesar in a pit filled with the bodies of horses, wild yaks, wild asses and men, over which she placed a flat stone. On this she placed three stones forming a tripod, and finally a container full of water. "Ho! Ho! I smell a man, I smell a dog. Has the Little Man of Tibet come?" asked the demon when he arrived. "Don't talk rubbish," replied the demoness, "the Little Man of Tibet has not arrived; you have just killed men and wild animals on the mountain. I have been here and I have not seen anything." "No doubt you are right," said the demon.

The next day the demon went off looking for Gesar. The demoness gave the keys of all the locks to Gesar, and indicated how to kill Dü Akyung: "You must hide yourself in the pit. When the demon has fallen asleep, two fishes with golden eyes, normally hidden in his hair, will emerge on his forehead. These fish are his *sog kyob*, the supports of his life-force, and they must be killed with an arrow."

When Dü Akyung came back, the demoness gave a bow and some arrows to Gesar. She hid him in the pit, which she covered with a flat stone on which she placed the tripod and lastly placed uppermost a basin filled with water. "Ho! Ho! I smell a man, I smell a dog. The Little Man of Tibet, has he arrived?" asked the demon.

The demoness said: "Don't talk nonsense, the Little Man of Tibet is not here. You have just killed men and wild

animals on the mountain and I have been in the house; I
have seen nothing."

"You are right," said the demon.

Gesar, hidden in the pit, tried to string the bow, but the
string slipped out of his hands and vibrated, making an
"*urting*" sound.

The demon then asked again: "The Little Man of Tibet,
has he not come?"

"It was my spindle that made the "*urting*" sound as it
was turning."

"Perhaps you are right," said the demon.

Uneasy, the demon made a divination.

"I have just performed a divination. The Little Man of
Tibet, who has taken on the appearance of a black stone, is
in a silo under a container of water," he told her.

"How is it possible for a man to hide under a container
full of water?" she asked.

"I want to stay awake. If I fall asleep, cry out Ha! Ha!
Ho! Ho!"

While the demon was dozing, the two golden fish, the
two supports of his life-force who lived in his hair, appeared on his forehead. Gesar came out of his hiding place,
drew the bow, took aim, and hit the two fishes, thus killing the demon.

To keep Gesar near her, the demoness gave him a potion to drink which caused him to forget his origin and
his past life.

The demoness used Gesar's horse for vile tasks. The
divine horse had to carry nine loads of human excrement
in the morning and nine more in the evening. The horse
worked so hard that soon running sores appeared over
each of his ninety-nine vertebrae.

Gesar stayed in the demon's house for nine years, nine
months and nine days without knowing it. One day, when
he was lying on his back, a white heron, sent by his wife
Shomodrugu of the land of Ling, flew over him and called
"*kikiro.*" Gesar did not hear it but some droppings of the bird
fell into his mouth and caused him to vomit the potion.

Gesar, regaining his senses, looked for his horse. He went to the east, to the south, to the west, to the north. He saw, near a spring, a horse covered with wounds, looking like a wild ass. The horse spoke to him with eyes full of tears: "You have abandoned me, you stayed here with a demoness and I have been forced to carry loads day after day. Can you imagine my misery?"

"Now you are free."

The horse rolled in the red earth near the spring and recovered instantly; his coat took the color of black and fawn and his mane became reddish ochre.

"Let us return to the land of Ling," said Gesar.

"As long as the demoness is alive, I will not leave this place," said the divine horse.

Gesar told the demoness that he was going to leave her, but she insisted on leaving with him.

Gesar flew in the sky with his horse; the demoness went by land with some goats, and they met again in the evening to pass the night together. This went on for three days.

"In order to go faster, leave your goats and mount on the rump behind me."

The horse, carrying Gesar and the demoness, flew up toward the sun and the moon, then came down again. The horse made every effort to shake off the demoness, who hung on by the tail. Finally, he made her release her hold over the sea, wherein she disappeared.

Gesar could then return to Ling.

The Identification of an Illegitimate Child

If you raise a young wolf, he will never be a watchdog.
If you adopt a child, he will never be your own.

Before we end our pilgrimage, we must still make a *nékhor* of the sacred mountain of Kula, the third important event in the *lingkhor* of Dolpo. Usually, one makes this round on the day of the full moon of the Seventh Month, that of the mid-summer. The trek from Tingkyu to Poldé takes two hours. From Poldé, we climb up to the temple of Balung, which is the point of departure for the *nékhor*. Here are found the imprints of the hands of Lama Balung Kunchog Yonten and the letters A and OM, spontaneously formed. The custodian of the temple, Namgyä, is a doctor trained by Mémé Tenzin from Kagar.

Kula is a *menri*, a mountain rich in medicinal plants. Namgyä, who accompanies us, can identify the medicinal plants and shows us the valerian, the rhizome of which is much sought after.

From the temple, the trail goes up in the direction of a little lake whose water has beneficial qualities. At the pass of Drolma, a moment of rest is very welcome. Standing against the *labtsé* of the pass, Karma takes his rosary and makes a divination.

Divinations are not always easy, as evidenced by the story that Karma then tells us. "Here is the story that I have heard, related by a man from Hor," Karma says.

A rich family lived on the border of China and Tibet. The parents had two sons and a third was born. But the mother died three days after the birth. The three sons were wise; the last born, however, was the most skillful in everything he undertook: archery, horse racing and all.

One day, their father called them together and told them: "I am going to die soon, but one of you, I do not know which one, is not my son. Therefore before my wealth is distributed, it will be necessary to establish which of you are my two real heirs. For this, it will be necessary to consult the king and his astrologer." And the father died not long after.

One day, the eldest said to his brothers: "This morning I am going hunting. Light the fire and prepare a good meal." Then he left. The second, seeing the eldest leave, said to himself: "Perhaps I am not to be an inheritor of this house. I am also going to hunt." And the third did the same.

Night came and the eldest, on his return, found the house empty. He was amazed but understood the thoughts of his brothers. He decided to consult the king on the subject of his origin.

On the way, he crossed a sandy plain where he noticed the imprints of two feet, two hands and a trace of liquid, perhaps urine. He thought about this, asking himself what this could mean. "Maybe it is a pregnant woman, ready to deliver, who has dragged herself this far?"

Continuing, he saw the imprints of feet, first pointing one way, then in the opposite direction. He thought, "This pregnant woman, without doubt, left after a quarrel with her husband, intending to return to her parents and then, along the way, she changed her mind."

A little further along he met a man who asked him: "Have you seen a woman on the sandy plain?"

"Is she pregnant?"

"Yes, she is going to deliver, but she has left home!" the man replied.

"You quarrelled with each other?" asked the eldest son, to which the man replied:

"Yes, she has gone. Where have you seen her?"

"In fact, I have not seen her," said the oldest son.

"How is this? At first you say that she is pregnant, and now you deny seeing her!"

"It was like this," said the young man. "I have thought about what I have seen and what I have told you is the result of my thoughts."

"I don't believe you," the man then said. "We must go to ask the opinion of the judge." Both went to find the judge. Accused of having killed the woman, the eldest son was thrown into prison.

One year later, the second brother, seeing that his elder brother did not return, left to make a visit to the king. On the way, he crossed a plain covered with a grassy pasture, where traces of a passing yak could be seen. As the grass was grazed on only one side of the trail that passed through the pasture, he thought: "Oh, the grass is grazed on only one side, the yak must be one-eyed." Then he noticed some red hair caught on the bushes and he thought: "This yak must have a red coat."

A little later, a man came to meet him, and asked: "Have you seen a yak?"

"Is the yak one-eyed, and with a red coat?" asked the second brother.

"Yes! Where have you seen it?" the man asked.

"In fact, I have not seen it," the second replied.

"Then how can you know that it is one-eyed and that it has red hair?"

"What I have said is the result of my thoughts," was his reply.

The two men went before the judge, one accusing the other of theft. The accused was thrown into prison.

One year later, the youngest brother, seeing that his elder brothers did not return, left in his turn to consult with

the king. Along the way, he entered a forest and saw under a tree on the right, a little honey, and under a tree on
the left, a little rice. He thought: "Well, well, a yak loaded
with a packsaddle has strayed into this thick forest. His
load on the right was of honey, his load on the left of rice.
And, since he was able to penetrate into this dense forest,
he probably did not have horns."

Further on, he met up with a driver of a caravan who
asked him: "Did you met a yak in the forest?"

"A yak *uril* with a load of rice and honey?" asked the
youngest brother.

"Indeed, that's the one!"

"In fact, I have not seen it," said the brother.

"How can you say that if you know even the nature of
the loads?"

"I have never seen your animal. What I say is the result
of my reasoning," replied the youngster.

But he was not believed and the two men went off to
see the judge, who threw the youngest brother into prison.

It was in this prison that the three brothers found themselves united again, and they recounted their adventures.
But as the wisdom of the three brothers was great, the judge
was not able to come to a decision about their guilt and so
they were sent to the king of the country.

Then the king put this question to the eldest: "How did
you guess that the woman was pregnant?"

"This woman, whose waters were breaking, no longer
had the strength to walk; she was dragging herself along
the ground."

"And why did you think there was a quarrel between
the husband and his wife?"

"Because of the coming and going of the footprints."

The king thought this man to be intelligent.

The second brother made known his adventures and
the king put this question to him: "How did you guess
that the yak was one-eyed?"

"The yak grazed the grass on only one side of the trail."

The third brother said that only a yak without horns could have penetrated the forest, and that a part of the contents of his loads had marked the two trees between which the yak had tried to pass.

The king stated that they were equally intelligent young men, and declared that they were innocent of the charges that had been made against them. He had the accusers locked up.

The brothers then said: "We three are brothers. Our mother died a long time ago and our father three years ago. Our father told us that one of us was not his son and advised us to see the king, to learn the truth of our origin."

Then the king made a divination in order to discover which of the three was the half-brother. However, the king was not able to get an answer from his divination, and he caused it to be proclaimed everywhere that whosoever could find the solution of the riddle would have part of the kingdom.

Ministers, sons of kings, soothsayers, astrologers and lamas came to see the three brothers and put a thousand questions to them without being able to identify the illegitimate one.

One day, a woman who sold beer thought: "One cannot ascertain the difference in the origin of the three brothers by looking at their faces or bodies, or by observing their intelligence, as they are so much alike. But their feelings may be different." Carrying a vessel of *arag*, she went to find the three brothers.

"I have just heard a story with an important meaning which is a riddle; I would like to understand it better," she said.

"Tell us this story and we will try to help you," they said.

And the woman related this story:

A long, long time ago, a king had a daughter. This girl, who was very intelligent, had as a playmate a boy of humble birth. After a while, the king's daughter said to the boy: "I want to be your wife; I will not marry anyone else."

The boy replied: "I am the son of a beggar, this will never be possible; everything is against us."

The girl boldly declared: "If I wish it, my parents will yield, and we will marry."

They then made a solemn promise to unite one day.

One day the king of a neighboring land asked for the king's daughter for his son. The father thought: "If I don't give my daughter to him, this powerful king will wage war on me." The girl refused, but her father insisted, saying: "If you do not accept, the king will wage war on us and destroy our kingdom."

The girl reflected: "All that is true, my parents will be killed and the kingdom will be destroyed." So at last she accepted the marriage. The king's daughter then confided to her mother: "A long time ago, I promised to marry the son of a beggar; what should I do?"

Her mother advised her to go and find him, and to come back the next day.

The girl, dressed in her most beautiful clothes, set out on a fine horse for the house of the poor lad. Along the way, seven thieves stopped her with the intention of taking her horse and her jewels.

"Free me, I promise to come back tomorrow and to give you everything that I have." The thieves let her go.

Arriving at the house of the poor boy, she said, "I have come to see you," and the boy rejoiced at her arrival.

"A long time ago, we were joined by a promise, but the son of a powerful king has demanded that I marry him, threatening to destroy my father's whole kingdom if I don't agree to be his wife. I come, therefore, to see you and to pass one night with you, as I promised."

"You cannot stay here with me tonight for, if the son of the king learns of it, he will kill me."

The girl assured him that he would not be killed, and spent the night with the boy. Before dawn, she said: "I am going now, don't be angry."

On the way, she found the seven thieves asleep. "Wake up, I have returned. If you want to kill me or take me as a wife, get on with it, then!"

The thieves thought: "Who is this woman who last night wished to save herself at any price and who now offers herself to us?"

"Who, then, are you?" they asked.

"I am the daughter of the king of this country!" she declared. One of the thieves said, "You are like a goddess." And they helped her to return to her parents.

Finally, the daughter of the king left for the neighboring kingdom and married there.

The eldest and the second brother listened to the story paying much attention and without saying anything. The youngest said: "Ha, Ha! These thieves, what sort of thieves are they? They have robbed and killed, but they have not killed the daughter of the king! They steal from the poor, but they do not steal from the king's daughter! The son of the poor man, what sort of a man is he? A girl comes to see him and he refuses to sleep with her! These thieves and this poor man have a way of behaving that is not normal!"

The woman who was trying to resolve the enigma then thought, "The third son has not the same ethical discipline nor way of thinking; he is different from the two others. He is the half-brother."

She announced her deductions to the king, who was convinced and rewarded her by giving her a part of his realm.

After the pass of Drolma, the path crosses two large meadows—"the little plain of the bird Khyung," and "the little plain of the White Lioness." Two springs flow nearby; one gives the "water of vitality," and the other one "pure water."

The Cow Ba-tratatrari

On the sixth day of the Sixth Month, a purchase will be to
  your advantage,
But if this day you sell something, there will be no profit.

The trail around Kula is very similar to the one around Shey, and Karma explains that it is also the same for the pilgrimage around Kang Tisé.

Late in the evening, at Tarka Sumdo, we rejoin the trail that links Tingkyu to Tarap. The confluence of the two streams is marked by a large *chörten*, which is known as the *"chörten* of many colors." We are overtaken by a boy and a girl of Poldé, grandchildren of Grandmother Angmo of Mondro in Tarap. Tarkyé, a very jovial fellow of thirty, is wearing red pants, a shirt of black cotton and a *chuba* of heavy cotton. His sister, Chonsom, wears baggy trousers of brown wool, a blouse of black cotton and a piece of multicolored fabric hanging down her back, held by a belt. At each stopping place, our companions eat a mixture of *tsampa* and butter; they gather the fallen crumbs in the folds of their *chuba*.

Below the last pass which leads to Tarap, a black tent has been erected at Sholung Sumna, in the middle of thickets of

caragana and dwarf willows. Our approach is met with furious barking, which is quickly stopped by the snapping of a sling.
This tent belongs to Kanglug, Karma's older brother, who
lives here with his family. Kanglug is four years older than
Karma. Dressed in a *chuba* of coarse wool, he never takes off
his felt hat. From time to time, he puts a little snuff on his thumb-
nail and slowly inhales it.

We occupy the places of honor, near the hearth. Karma, sa-
voring curds and tea, retraces, with the art of the storyteller
that he is, the days of our travels and the most important events,
recalling at length the mummy of Shang Rinpoché, as well as
the anxiety of the villagers of Shimen and Tingkyu regarding
the present conditions of grain-salt barter with Tibet.

The tent is guarded by an unusually large mastiff. Karma
draws my attention to the yellow hair in the dog's eyebrows.
These signify that the dog has the power of scaring away demons coming near the encampment at night. The hairs of the
dog also have another advantage: when the ears of little girls
are pierced, a few hairs are inserted into the holes to hasten
their healing.

Seated near the hearth, I ask Karma for a story about the
Great Plain of the North.

On the grasslands of Changtang, an old woman was
living with a single son and a little calf, Ba-tratatrari. It
happened that one day they were without food or money.
The son went off to the east to hunt, taking, for magic
power, some black and white dust. He walked for seven
days, then for twenty-one days.

Arriving at Shar Panglung, he saw in the distance an
antelope. He approached quietly and scattered a little black
dust under the antelope, who was bedded down. This
caused the antelope to become stuck to the ground.

"Little Man of Tibet, why have you trapped me?" the
animal asked.

"I have an old mother who is dying of hunger and she
has asked me to bring her some meat," replied the son.

"Little Man of Tibet, let me go and I will furnish you with meat."

The boy sprinkled a little of the white dust, thus freeing the animal, who, by magic power, gave him a large amount of meat.

Returning to the tent with the load of meat, he made the tent stay vibrate, which emitted the sound *"urting-urting."*

"Mother, I have come back with a quantity of meat!"

Another day, the mother noticed that the stock of salt was exhausted, and sent her son out for some more. The boy left in a northerly direction and arriving at Tsari, he saw many wild yaks. Going closer to the place where these animals customarily slept, he scattered a little of the black dust. When the largest of the yaks bedded down, he became stuck to the earth.

"Little Man of Tibet, what do you want? Why do you want to kill me?" asked the yak.

"I have an old mother who has need of salt from the great salt lake of the North," said the boy.

"Free me, and I will give you a load of salt, for I am the guardian of the salt," said the yak.

Throwing a little of the white dust, the boy freed the yak, who brought him a large amount of salt.

During this time, the mother lamented, not seeing her son return. Then, all at once she heard the stay vibrate *"urting-urting,"* and rejoiced at the sight of the load of salt.

After a while, the old woman exhausted her supply of raw sugar and raisins. The son left again, walking for a long time in a southerly direction, and he arrived in Yari, the land of blue cliffs. In a small valley he saw a herd of wild sheep with large horns. He approached their resting place, scattered a little of the black dust and thus captured the most handsome of the males.

"Little Man of Tibet, why have you trapped me? What do you want?"

"My mother has exhausted her supplies of raw sugar and raisins," said the boy.

"Free me and I will show you how to get supplies."

The boy freed the animal with a little of the white dust and returned to the tent with a heavy load of sugar and raisins.

But the old woman was lacking *tsampa* and so the son set out again, this time toward the west.

Having walked for a long time, he saw some wild asses, *kyang,* running in all directions; he threw a bit of the black dust in their path and caught one.

"Little Man of Tibet, why do you capture me?"

"My old mother needs *tsampa* and sent me in the direction of the west."

"Free me and I will get you plenty of *tsampa!*"

The son returned to the tent, causing the stay to vibrate, *"urting-urting,"* and the mother was delighted with the load of *tsampa* that he brought.

"Mother, we now have the treasures of the Four Directions: the treasure of the East, meat given by the antelope; the treasure of the North, salt given by the wild yak; the treasure of the South, raw sugar and raisins given by the wild sheep; and the treasure of the West, *tsampa,* given by the wild ass."

Later, being again without resources, the boy decided to steal a yak from the courtyard of a rich neighbor.

The cow, Ba-tratatrari, because she was a deity, guessed the boy's intention and said to him: "Child, don't commit the sin of stealing. Kill me rather than steal."

"Why should I kill you? Is this not an even more grave sin?"

"As I am a deity, you do not commit a sin by killing me. I will assume another form and my body will transform into precious substances. After killing me, stretch the skin flat with the head oriented toward the east and the tail toward the west. Throw my front feet toward the north, my vertebrae to the south, my back feet toward the east. Throw my head toward the cliff; my lungs toward the mountain; the contents of my belly on the plain; the hairs toward the sky; my kidneys and intestines in the water. As for my tail, present it to someone."

The boy followed the advice of the cow. He killed her, cut her up and disposed of all the pieces in the way he was told to do.

Awakening the next morning, the boy saw only marvels! At the place where the skin had been stretched, there was a beautiful three-storied house. The front feet were transformed into warriors. The head had become turquoises. The vertebrae had become all kinds of trees. The lungs had become large rocks of various colors. The contents of the belly had become excellent pasture. The hairs had become stars in the heavens. The intestines had turned into pebbles, polished by a river. The back feet had become many herds and the tail had produced lineages of powerful men!

Thanking the cow that had given so much wealth, the boy prayed to the Buddhas of the Three Times[38] and gave food to those who were in need.

We come out of the tent for a last time. Kanglug unchains the dog, who disappears into the night. Back in the tent, we go to sleep, pressed one against the other, on a blanket of yak hair, heads resting lightly on a tilted plank which serves as a pillow.

The Return to Kagar

Tarap is like a silken ornament,
And Dolpo the garment it decorates.

We leave the encampment at sunrise and make the ascent of Tso-la, passing the little glacial lake situated below the pass. We advance laboriously over the broken schist that makes walking so arduous, and rain, mixed with snow, overtakes us at more than 4,900 meters. After crossing the pass we descend rapidly into the small valley of Shulag. Here, Lama Pargö had lived, a saintly man whose story Karma relates to us as we walk.

Pargö was born in western Tibet, near the sacred Kang Tisé, the axis of the world. His father was a chieftain of the region and lived in a three-story palace. His mother, it is said, carried him for fifteen months, which was a good omen.

At the age of one, Pargö appeared to be three; at three years he appeared to be seven, but gradually, as he grew older, his ill nature and naughtiness increased. He bullied the girls, beat up his playmates, threw stones at dogs, hurt the lambs and the kids, pulled the tails of yaks, all without any reason. At the age of sixteen, he went to Dolpo

with a caravan and quarrelled with the villagers during the traditional barter of salt and barley. At the Pangong-la, he even forgot the ritual of burning incense to the divinities guarding the pass!

One day, he killed a partridge with his sling; a little later he was stricken with leprosy. All his body was covered with scars, and, ashamed, he hid himself in a cave. His mother came to find him there, advised him to repent, and gave him her blessing. Pargö, confused in his mind, stayed voluntarily as a recluse. But one day a lama, Jatang, an incarnation of the Buddha Dorjechang, visited him and instructed him in the Religion, and a miraculous cure occurred! Jatang gave Pargö the name of Bumpal, but for us, he is a *togden*, rich in learning and understanding.

Pargö entered religious life after having meditated for three years, three months, and three days. He then went south and set himself up at Balung where he built a small temple.

Thirteen times he made the *nékhor* of the mountain, the route since established as the pilgrimage of Kula. He then built the temple of Trolung in the valley of the Panzang. Pargö knew magic spells which enabled him to transport very heavy stones without effort. He easily did the work of ten men, but had forbidden his helpers to watch him produce these results. One day, when an overly curious worker saw Pargö carry a very heavy rock, he left it midway at a place called Polung Yujab. Thus he constructed many temples, among them that of Penri. He meditated at Sharing, where a monk had given him hospitality. The wife of his host wanted to lie with him. At night, the woman came near to Pargö, groaning *"uchu, uchu"*[39]; Pargö, not understanding her real meaning, gave her his clothes.[40] But the woman was insistent, so Pargö fled, naked, into the night.

Pargö built temples in the four valleys of Dolpo. Meditating in a cave, near the spring "where the fairies dance," each night he saw, always at the same place, a little lamp glittering. One day, he asked his servant to empty the urinal at the place where he had seen the lamp burning. The urine vaporized before touching the earth, and from this Pargö concluded that the place should not be defiled. He decided to construct a temple there with the help of the villagers of Tarap and called it Mekyem.

Pargö died on the tenth day of the Eighth Month, an auspicious day, and his body remained in the position of meditation for ten days. After cremation, his heart, his tongue and his eyes were found intact. They were then enshrined in a gilded *chörten* placed on the altar in Mekyem.

Pargö had great power, and he gave the villagers a blessing in written form to obtain good harvests. But after three generations, the chief of the village threw this sheet of paper into the fire, and since that time, the harvests in Tarap have been poor.

Pargö also revealed some special *mantras* providing protection from hailstorms, spells still in the possession of a lineage of lamas in the valley.

From the terraced fields of Uri, we are able to see the valley of Tarap, where the barley is just visible. It's another two more hours of easy walking before we reach Kagar. On the way there are conversations with Chögya at Karwa and at Tango with old Lhamo, who showed much curiosity. And, at last, here is Kagar!

As Kagar Rinpoché is celebrating the ritual of the Tenth Day, we put off our visit till the next day and go directly to Karma's tent.

Lhaki has changed the location of the tent; it is now on the right bank of the Tarap River, a little higher up. She waits for us at the side of the tent, restraining the dog by his red collar in the way that is characteristic of *drogpa* women.

The beer of welcome is ready and the tent is too small to contain everyone. The flaps of the entry have been lifted to enlarge the circle of those who have come to hear Karma relate a new story. He hangs his sling on the pole, above the hearth, and places his reliquary on a shelf. Has he kept this story for the end? I do not know, but one senses that he especially loves it:

This took place a very long time ago. The faithful maidservant of the king Serla Gon had a son. When the son was fifteen years old, his mother died and he became the king's shepherd.

The king had three daughters; the oldest bore the name of Serlo, "Leaf-of-gold"; the second, the name Ngulo, "Leaf-of-silver"; and the youngest, Dunglo, "Leaf-the-color-of-conch."

The son of the maidservant, in truth, was the son of a deity. He had no hair, his skull was covered with turquoises, gold, silver and pearls. But these jewels were invisible to the eyes of his companions, who only saw beeswax on his head; hence came his surname Yoklari: "Servant with the bald head covered with beeswax."

One day, the king decided to marry off his three daughters. He brought together all the people, and said: "The two older daughters will have a kingdom to share, the youngest will have my kingdom."

The king, having brought together all the chieftains of the land, asked each of the daughters to choose a husband. The chieftains had dressed in their most beautiful costumes and were mounted on their finest horses. The eldest daughter made her choice first. Carrying a little butter in her left hand, and in her right hand a flag with the five auspicious colors, she chose the son of the king of the country to the South; she planted the flag in front of the chosen one, and put butter on his forehead.

The middle daughter, in her turn, planted her banner before the son of the king of the West and dabbed butter, the symbol of good fortune, on his forehead.

The last girl, Dunglo, looked over all the assembled princes. She went to the right, then to the left, hesitating, without planting the flag she had in her hand. The king, seeing her hesitate, said to her: "Make your choice. Whoever you decide on, I will accept your decision, for I am a powerful king and everyone obeys me."

The daughter then made her choice; she planted her flag in front of Yoklari, the young servant of the king, and put butter on his forehead, the symbol of good fortune.

The king spoke out in anger: "This choice is useless, you are deceiving yourself."

But the queen said: "This choice, without doubt, is good because it is my daughter who has made it. It is the choice of her heart."

The king, furious, gave nothing to his youngest daughter. However, to the two older girls he gave a fabulous dowry of gold, silver and precious stones. To Dunglo he gave only an old lame mare and a small tent made of shreds of faded colors. Thus equipped, Yoklari and his wife departed for a distant destination.

One month after the marriage ceremonies, the king's sons-in-law, the husbands of the two older daughters, came to visit their father-in-law, according to the custom followed in *drogpa* land. The king had looked forward to the celebrations. There would be archery, wrestling, and horse racing. Yoklari also arrived and he erected his tattered tent near the palace, but the king made it known to him that he did not want to see him nor talk to him.

Dunglo visited her mother, carrying salt in her hand. Yoklari had told her: "Take a fistful of salt, you eat a very little of it, as if you were crunching a louse, you throw a little salt into the fire, and the salt bursts in the fire like a louse. They will think that we are poor and covered with lice."

"My beloved daughter, how are you getting along?" asked the queen.

"Mother, I have no clothes and I am covered with lice."

The queen gave a costume to her daughter which Yoklari gave to a poor person.

During the visit of the sons-in-law, the king decided to bequeath his kingdom to the winner of three competitions to be held in a year's time: horse racing, archery and musket shooting.

Yoklari went back to the country Shar Panglung Kama, where he erected his tent and put his old mare out to graze. Now, on the tenth day of the First Month, a male colt was born to this over-aged mare.

The following year, the king made it known that the horse races would be held in the center of the kingdom. Dunglo said to Yoklari: "Now it is time to reveal your true identity, to show your head covered with gold and precious stones."

Yoklari arrived first and erected a tent of extraordinary whiteness, as large as ten of the largest tents known. Numerous servants attended him, but he did not make himself known. The other two sons-in-law of the king also arrived.

The king was surprised that Yoklari did not arrive. He wanted to hasten the race, but the queen insisted that the third son-in-law also be present. Seven men, then, went out in search of Yoklari. Seven days later, they had not yet found him.

By the large plain, the white tent of the rich trader had been much noticed and close by was the old tent and the old mare which had been given to Yoklari. The king decided to send a messenger to the trader to investigate.

"Who are you? Are you king or trader? My master would like to know."

"I am a trader from China. I have no reason to see the king. I am more powerful than he is and a hundred times richer," said Yoklari.

The messenger reported to the king, but he had seen neither the old tent nor the old mare.

The king, curious, went himself to examine the tent of the rich trader, accompanied by some ministers and his two sons-in-law. Yoklari was seated on a golden throne in this tent; the daughter Dunglo, on a throne of turquoise. At the arrival of the king, a servant wished to offer him a throne of gold, but Yoklari said: "This king has no right to a golden throne; give him a tiger skin."

"What is the nature of your business?" asked the king.

"Have you not seen in your land a man with a head covered with beeswax, with a young wife, an old mare, and an old tent?"

"We have no knowledge of anything similar to this," said Yoklari.

"What is your lineage?"

"I was born in China," replied Yoklari.

"And your wife, what is her lineage?"

"I do not exactly know, but she comes from the land of the West." The girl hid part of her face behind her sleeve of silk.

The king then said: "Tomorrow, a horse race will take place. My three sons-in-law must participate in it. As the third has not come, and we have searched everywhere for

him, I ask you, as a sign of good fortune, to participate in
the race. Besides, I will buy much merchandise from you."
And the king went off with his companions.

The next day, Yoklari presented himself to the king, his
head coated with beeswax, the wife dressed in scraps, followed by the old mare and the colt. The maidservant of
the queen saw them come, and announced the news to
her mistress: "Yoklari is here! The old mare has had a colt!"
The king was immediately informed.

The race was to take place at midday. The two elder
sons-in-law each entered seven horses, with seven riders.
Yoklari rode the young colt.

The fourteen horsemen of the elder sons-in-law were
dressed in rich costumes of silk; Yoklari was wearing an
old torn jacket, almost completely eaten away. The king
announced the competitions of the day: horse racing, archery, and musket shooting. "The winner will receive the
jewel *Gondö Punjung*, my throne and my kingdom," he said.

The race then took place. The riders took off at a gallop,
but the colt of Yoklari did not want to run, he went slowly,
gently, haltingly, carrying his rider with difficulty. All at
once, Yoklari was seen to overtake, colt and rider astride a
rainbow. The fourteen horsemen quarrelled at the finish,
each believing that he was the winner. The king, who had
seen the rider on the rainbow, thought: "This Yoklari can
only be the incarnation of a deity." Yoklari, who had won
the race, received the jewel.

At archery, Yoklari, still in rags, won, having pierced a
silver coin at the very center of the target.

For the musket shooting, Yoklari put on his most beautiful clothes, his head appearing ornamented with turquoises and precious stones. The king was so astonished
at this that he could not open his mouth.

The sons-in-law demanded: "Who is this great prince?
Is this Yoklari?" They assumed this because of the presence of the young colt. All the assembled people recognized Yoklari. His appearance was so extraordinary that
the shooting competition was forgotten. Yoklari then pre-

sented himself as the king of Shar Panglung Kama and invited the king, his father-in-law, and the queen to come and visit him.

The two elder daughters of the king, wishing to get an idea of their sister's wealth, went, disguised as beggars, to Shar Panglung Kama. Dunglo, having guessed the identity of the beggars, gave them a large number of gifts. The girls, upon returning, told the story of their adventure, saying: "Yoklari is seated on a golden throne; Dunglo on a throne of turquoise; the attendants are richly clothed; their palace is of coral."

The king and queen came to visit their son-in-law, who received them in royal style. The king questioned Yoklari about his origin and lineage: "I am the son of a deity; this is the reason for my wealth in gold and turquoise."

Yoklari gave his father-in-law many presents, seven mule-loads of precious stones, seven loads of raw sugar and raisins, and seven loads of Chinese silk. And at his father-in-law's death, Yoklari became king.

Karma is worn out. Lhaki offers tea all around.

I ponder on the horseman of the divine white horse; on the *tsen*; on the owner of turquoise treasures; on the quest for the impossible. In Karma's mind, where does reality stop, where does the imaginary begin?

The End of the Pilgrimage

The mountain peaks that dominate the valley of Tarap are covered with snow: "rain and snow in summer; winter cold and rough," according to a Dolpo proverb.

Everyone in Kagar joins in the preparations for our meeting with Kagar Rinpoché. He receives us in his chapel. After he touches our heads with his prayer-wheel in blessing, we offer him a white scarf with a silver coin wrapped in a corner, a dish of *tsampa* decorated with three bits of butter, some roots of valerian gathered on the Kula mountain, roses from the hermitage above Po and crystals of quartz from the mountain of Shey.

Karma takes out the turquoise that has protected us and touches it to his forehead. He hands it to Kagar Rinpoché, who polishes it with a fold of his *chuba*. Kagar Rinpoché looks at it for a long time, then puts it back in a reliquary kept on the altar. How many times has this sacred turquoise made a tour of the places sacred to the people of Dolpo? How many times will it do this again?

Yangzom comes into the room carrying a vessel containing excellent beer. We hold out our bowls. Karma rolls out his report and Yangzom brings a second vessel. Rinpoché counts his rosary and corrects some of Karma's remarks.

The announcement *Nékhorwa lepsong,* "The pilgrims are back," has been made round the village and the room is filled with friends and neighbors.

Karma tells of the places we visited and his account is already a story!

Listening to Karma, another story comes to my mind, one I had first heard as a young researcher in Sikkim. I had witnessed the trance of a Lepcha healer who was curing a patient and I wanted to obtain from him the source of his knowledge. Which books was it from? Which scriptures? What are the formal and written sources? I was desperate to find a written source. Without a material and durable reference, I doubted the efficacy of the ritual.

To my questions, repeated with the artlessness of one who was convinced that an effective cure must have a reference in a written document, the intercessor eventually replied:

A long time ago, Lord Buddha decided to distribute wisdom to mankind. All the people of the land came to the assembly; the Tibetans, the Bhutanese, the men of the mountains, the men of the valleys, and the Lepcha, my ancestors.

The Tibetans, tall, strong and confident, took all the books, and my Lepcha ancestor was able to obtain only one letter of the alphabet. Not knowing what to do with it, but knowing that it was sacred, he swallowed it.

After the others had left, Lord Buddha came near to my ancestor, who was sitting alone and dejected, and asked him the reason for his sadness.

"The Tibetans have taken all the wisdom; I have received only a single letter of the alphabet," he said.

"The Tibetans have wisdom in their books; you, Lepcha, you have Wisdom in your heart," replied Lord Buddha.

Notes

1. Mount Kailash, also known in Tibet as Kang Rinpoché.

2. Champa (Sanskrit, Maitreya), the embodiment of the loving-kindness of all the buddhas, is said to be the next Buddha to come to this world.

3. The Jowo statue in Lhasa represents Buddha Shakyamuni as a young prince.

4. The Great Black One (Sanskrit, Mahakala), is a protector deity considered to be a wrathful manifestation of the Buddha of Compassion, Avalokiteshvara.

5. Three Jewels of Buddhism: Buddha, Dharma, and Sangha.

6. Sanskrit, Garuda.

7. A dwarf.

8. The Pleiades play an important role in Tibetan beliefs.

9. Each face of the knuckle-bones is identified with one of six animals.

10. Questions are posed mentally and the answers appear on the bone in the form of one or more fine cracks and splits.

11. "The falling drops," i.e., it's raining.

12. "Make love."

13. *Chachatiwa.*

14. *Chochichi.*

15. This dust has magic powers; the black dust causes the body to adhere to the ground; the white frees it. This form of magic recurs in other fables.

16. Sanskrit, Vajradhara. This is the form the Buddha takes when teaching tantras.

17. The lotus is the emblem of Drolma (Sanskrit, Tara), the Savioress.

18. The Three Protectors (Rigsum Gompo): Jampelyang (Sanskrit, Manjushri), Chenrezi (Sanskrit, Avalokiteshvara) and Chanadorjé (Sanskrit, Vajrapani).

19. Padmasambhava.

20. When a mare has a foal, the little one always follows the mother.

21. In Tibet there are two religions—Buddhism (called *chö*) and Bön. In Dolpo also the two coexist.

22. *Dö* (Tib., *mdo*) refers to the sutras, the canonical collection of texts spoken by the Buddha (Kanjur); *Yüm* refers to the Prajnaparamita, or Perfection of Wisdom, sutras, known as the "mother" (Tib., *yum*) of wisdom.

23. The Tibetan New Year is determined by the lunar calendar and is the occasion for numerous rituals. One of these is the preparation of a soup of nine ingredients: barley, wheat, rice, cheese, roots of potentilla, bamboo shoots, peas, mutton and salt.

24. "Without horns."

25. The Kanjur is the canonical collection of texts spoken by the Buddha; the Tanjur is the canonical collection of authoritative commentarial writings by subsequent Indian masters.

26. This statement is highly blasphemous. Unknown to the *drogpa,* Chang Apa's words have a double meaning, equating the pole with the basic tenets of Buddhism.

27. *Khandro* (Sanskrit, *dakini*), literally "sky-goers," are said to work either for good or for evil, never both.

28. Machig, the Mother, was a disciple of a famous Indian yogi (Dampa Sangyé, 1062-1160 AD) and founder of a tantric school in Tibet.

29. One of the most frequently recited liturgic texts in the Nyingma tradition.

30. Opamé: Sanskrit, Amitabha; the buddha of pure perception. Chenrezi: Sanskrit, Avalokiteshvara; the buddha of compassion.

31. Lake Manasarovar.

32. Sanskrit: *Om Ah Hum Vajra Guru Padma Siddhi Hum.*

33. "Simple Minded."

34. "Much Insolence."

35. In the Tibetan calendar, the Year of the Bird, which occurs every twelve years, is the best year to make the circuit of the holy places in the Kathmandu Valley.

36. Pleiades.

37. On the left bank of the Yarlung Tsangpo, not far from Lhasa.

38. Buddhas of the past, present and future.

39. "I'm cold, I'm cold."

40. In Tibet, before going to sleep, one undresses completely, and covers oneself with one's clothes and a blanket, spread one over the other.

Bibliographical Notes

The legendary accounts and tales, as well as the themes illustrated by Karma, are inherited from a fund of pan-Tibetan popular folk tales, with which the Western world is now familiar through the many written versions that have already been published, first in the Tibetan language, then translated and commented upon.

These themes, which recur frequently in the stories, were largely borrowed from the ancient fund of Indian folklore, having found a place in the literature of the Buddhist canon where they are sanctified in several volumes of the Kanjur. However, the cultural context and the details in the presentations are wholly Tibetan: the vertical topographic divisions of a valley into "high," "low," and "middle"; the horizontal topographic divisions of East, West and the Middle; the passes which are difficult to climb over and go beyond; the numerous fords; the structure of the house and the tent; and the merry-making—archery, horse races, wrestling, songs and dances—without which festivals are not sanctified or rendered valid.

Myths of origin are numerous in Tibet, and have been linked to pre-Buddhist beliefs. In Bön tradition, the ancestor of humanity is born of a hailstone, and this belief is also found among the Nepali populations of the Tibeto-Burman languages and cultures. Similarly, among the Thakali of Nepal, the Bata Chan clan is considered to be born of a black yak, itself born to a devotee who had swallowed a hailstone.

In some of the stories, the heroes make use of magic objects and procedures, which make it easier to procure all manner of desirable items, such as the whip that leads to where one wants to go; a lucky bag that feeds when food is desired; a hat that makes the wearer invisible (Stein, 1959).

The story of the Demon Atsing and the girl Somaki, as well as that of the "Horseman who does not steal or lie," form a part of a series of tales known in Tibetan as *ro-drung,* the stories of the Corpse (Tales of the Vetala) (MacDonald, 1967). The narrative of the witch and her son who is saved by Ralotsawa is included in the biography of Ralopa (David-Neel, 1952).

The pranks of Chang-Apa are similar to both those of Aku Tonpa, the deceitful (although Karma has, indeed, stressed the difference that exists between these two characters), as well as to those of the saintly prankster Drukpa Kunleg (Stein, 1972).

In particular, the epic of the hero Gesar, for which we are much indebted to the scholarly works of R.A. Stein, is known throughout the Tibetan world. It exists in a written form and professional bards relate its episodes, and episodes have recently been made into a serial for television! The story of the battle between Gesar and the demon Akyung is one of the most frequently heard tales among the *drogpa* of western Tibet (Stein, 1959, 1962; Helffer, 1977).

Bibliographical References

Asboe, W. "A Thousand Tibetan Proverbs." *Journal of the Royal Asiatic Society* 8 (Paris, 1942).

Bacot, J. *La conversion du chasseur.* Paris: Études d'Orientalisme, 1932.

——. *Trois mystères tibétains.* Paris, 1921.

Bull, G. *Tibetan Tales.* London: Hodder and Staughton, 1969; Paris: Editions Grund, 1974.

Conze, E. *The Buddha's Law Among the Birds.* Oxford, 1955.

David-Neel, A. *Textes tibétains.* Paris, 1952.

Duncan, M.H. *Harvest Festival Dramas of Tibet.* Hong Kong, 1955.

——. *Love Songs and Proverbs of Tibet.* London, 1951.

Francke, A.H. "Die Geschichten des toten No-rub-can." *Zeitschrift der Deutschen Morgenlandischen Gesellschaft* 75 (1921).

——. *Geistesleben in Tibet.* Gütersloh, 1925.

Gordon, A.K. *Tibetan Tales.* London, 1952.

Helffer, M. *Les chants dans l'epopée tibétaine du Ge-sar d'après le livre de la course du chaval, version de Blo-bzaṅ bsTan-'jin.* Paris-Geneve, 1977.

Hermanns, M. *Himmelsstier und Gletscherlowe, Mythen, Sagen, und Fabeln aus Tibet,* Eisenach Kassel, 1955.

——. *Mythen und Mysterien, Religion und Magie der Tibeter.* Cologne, 1955.

Hoffmann, H. *Geschichte Tibets.* Munich, 1954.

——. *Marchen aus Tibet,* Düsseldorf-Köln, 1965.

Hyde-Chambers, F. and A. *Tibetan Folk Tales.* Boulder: Shambhala, 1981.

Jest, C. *Dolpo, communautés de langue tibétaine du Népal.* Paris: CNRS, 1974.

——. *Tarap, une vallée dans l'Himalaya.* Paris: Le Seuil, 1974.

Lal Keshar. *Lore and Legends of Nepal.* Nagapur, 1961.

Lalou, M. *Les religions du Tibet.* Paris, 1957.

Large-Blondeau, A.M. "Les pelerinages tibétains." *Les Pelerinages. Sources orientales* (Paris, 1960): 203-245.

——. *La vie de Pema Obar.* Paris, 1973.

Leitner, M. *Tibetanische Marchen.* Berlin, 1923.

Lüders, H. and E. *Buddhistische Marchen.* (Marchen der Weltliteratur.) Jena, 1922.

MacDonald, A.W. *Matériaux pour l'étude de la littérature populaire tibétaine.* 2 vols. Paris, 1967-72.

MacDonald, D. "Tibetan Tales." *Folklore* 42 (1931).

O'Connor, W.F. *Folktales from Tibet.* London, 1906.

Rinjing, D. *Tales of Uncle Tompa.* San Rafael, 1975.

Sakya, K., and L. Griffith. *Tales of Kathmandu: Folktales from the Himalayan Kingdom of Nepal.* 2nd ed. Kathmandu: Mandala Book Point, 1992.

Snellgrove, D.L. *Four Lamas of Dolpo, Autobiographies of Four Tibetan Lamas* (15th-18th centuries). 2 vols. Oxford, 1967-78.

Snellgrove, D.L., and H.E. Richardson. *A Cultural History of Tibet.* London, 1968.

Stein, R.A. *La civilisation tibétaine.* Paris, 1962; 1981.

——. *L'épopée tibétain de Gesar dans sa version lamaique de Ling,* Paris, 1956.

——. *Recherches sur l'épopée et le barde au Tibet.* Paris, 1959.

———. *Vie et chants de 'Brug-pa Kun-legs le yogin.* Paris, 1972.

Thomas, F.W. *Ancient Folk-literature from North-eastern Tibet.* Berlin, 1957.

Thurlow, C. *Stories from Beyond the Clouds: An Anthology of Tibetan Folk Tales.* Dharamsala: Library of Tibetan Works and Archives, 1975.

Waddell, L.A. *The Buddhism of Tibet or Lamaism.* London, 1895; Cambridge, 1958.

Glossary

Agu	uncle
Ajo	elder brother
Aka	exclamation of pain or surprise
ambag	internal "pocket" of *chuba*
amchi	doctor
apso	long-haired dog
arag	distilled liquor
Bö gi michung	"Little Man of Tibet," nickname of Ling Gesar
bumpa	vase
bushugsa	"the place where one begs for a son"
Champa	Sanskrit, Maitreya
chagsowa	blacksmith
chang	beer
chörten	shrine, reliquary; Sanskrit, stupa
chu	water, river
chuba	form of dress
do	lower part of the valley
dobdob	monk in charge of discipline
dorjé	thunderbolt, ritual object
dre	ghost
dremo	witch
dri	female of yak

drogpa	nomadic herder
Drolma	Sanskrit, Tara
drong	wild yak
dü	demon
dümo	demoness
dzo	crossbreed of yak and cow
Gompo	Sanskrit, Mahakala
gompa	temple, monastery
gönyer	temple caretaker
gyadrong	"100 houses," i.e., large villa
Kang Tisé	Tibetan name for Mount Kailash
karma	star
karma mindrug	"six stars," Pleiades
khandro	Sanskrit, *dakini;* female beings. There are many classes of *khandro:* human, emanations of Buddhas, or witches. The first two act for good, the third for evil.
khangpa	house
khata	ceremonial scarf made of white gauze
khorlam	circumambulation
Khyung	Sanskrit, Garuda; mythical bird
Kunchog sum	The Triple Jewel of Buddhism, represents the three jewels of refuge—in Sanskrit, Buddha, Dharma and Sangha.
kurim	religious ceremony to stop or avert illness, defilement, danger
kyang	wild ass
la	vital spirit, life-force, ability to function, will to live
la-yü	a turquoise that protects the vital spirit, a talisman
labtsé	cairn
leutor	sacrificial cake representing the *lu*
lha	divinity of the heavens
lhamdrog	strap used for tying up Tibetan boots
lhapa	medium
lharta	divine horse
lharta karpo	divine white horse

lhechen kachen	a gifted person for whom all tasks are easy
Lho-ling	"country to the south"
lingkhor	a long pilgrimage with visits to several sacred places
lu	Sanskrit, *naga*; divinity of the sub-soil, springs, and lakes
lung	wind
lungta	prayer flag, lit. "wind horse"
manipa	teller of religious stories
mantra	religious or magical formulas or invocation
mé	fire
mendang	prayer wall
menri	mountain rich in medicinal plants
mo gyab	divination
ngagpa	magician, religious practitioner of great power
nékhor	pilgrimage within a small area
norbu	jewel
norbu chushel	"water crystal jewel"
Nub-ling	"country of the West"
pachen	soothsayer
par	middle
po-lha	ancestor gods
rapo	he-goat
Rinpoché	precious; title and term of respectful address for certain lamas
rolang	zombie, walking corpse
ruchung	people of low social strata
sa	earth
sadag	divinities of the soil
se pug	"cave of roses"
sera shungkhen	lama who stops hail
sertrang	gold coin
Shar Panglung Kama	"East Pasture Variegated"
shidag gi khorlo	"almanac of the local divinities"
sog kyob	life-protecting object
taka	knuckle-bone
tashi sol	benediction

tashing	element of a loom
tangka	religious painting on cloth
tigi	foal
tingsha	cymbal
tö	upper part, west
to-u trug mug tug to to	onomatopoeic sound
togchag	meteorite
togden	one who has gained deep stable insights and realizations
tolwa	metal worker
torma	sacrificial moldings
towo	three stones placed atop one another
trag maryang	reddish cliff
trutob	tantric practioner who has achieved actual attainments (yogic powers)
tsampa	roasted barley flour
tsen	divinity of the intermediate world
tsipa	person who practices divination
tso	lake
Tso Mapam	Lake Manasarovar
tugpo	ram
tulku	incarnate
u-yu	without horns
uma	upper part of a settlement
uril	without horns
urlu	element of a loom
"*urting-urting*"	sound of cord snapping
urtu	sling
yang-gam	box of good augury
yidam	tutelary deity
yü	turquoise
yul-lha	a local deity
zi	agate bead with special bands